# Leicester
# MURDERS

## Ben Beazley

The
History
Press

Published in the United Kingdom in 2008 by
Sutton Publishing, an imprint of The History Press

Reprinted in 2010 by
The History Press
The Mill, Brimscombe Port
Stroud, Gloucestershire, GL5 2QG
www.thehistorypress.co.uk

British Library Cataloguing in Publication Data
A catalogue record for this book is available from the British
Library.

ISBN 978 0 7509 4810 4

Typesetting and origination by
The History Press Ltd

# CONTENTS

# INTRODUCTION

Any collection of murders, such as those contained in this volume, needs to be put into the context of the resources available at the time when the murders were committed. With this in view, I have set out in the following pages a brief outline of the detective department which was established in the early years of the Leicester Borough Police, evolving later into the Criminal Investigation Department (CID) of the City Police, along with some comments on the forensic assistance to which they had access.

In many of the cases, while the circumstances of the crime may not have been in dispute, the decisions reached by both judges and juries can be somewhat perplexing. A man deliberately cuts the throat of a two-year-old child (Arnold Warren, 1914), and the jury recommends leniency, 'because the crime was not long planned'. In a gangland dispute, the killer armed with a .45 revolver seeks out his victim and deliberately shoots him – not once, but twice in the body, and is found guilty of manslaughter (George Buxton, 1944). For this reason, where available, details of the trial and the judge's summing up – which essentially guides the jury to make their ultimate decision – are available, they are included. Perhaps surprisingly over time, there is in a variety of ways a consistency which has led to many of these decisions becoming what in law are known as 'cases stated', and are used in the present day by the legal profession as benchmarks upon which to base decisions.

The first case reviewed is that concerning the murder in 1832 of John Paas by James Cook. This crime was particularly chosen because, in the days prior to the existence of any organised police system, it is the last of its kind in the Leicester Borough to be investigated by an officer of the local authority – the town clerk, Thomas Burbidge. Not only did this occur at a time when there was no police force as such in existence, but also, any proposal to create one was viewed by both the good and the bad with a deal of opposition. This attitude was based very much on the fact that a police force had for some time been in existence in France, where it was universally regarded with suspicion due to its oppressive nature, and as often in modern times, dedicated more to spying on the individual rather than on the detection of crime. (As in Germany during the period when Hitler's Third Reich was in power, the Gestapo and Sicherheitsdienst were used as a means of instilling terror and obedience into the everyday life of Germans, as were the various secret police organisations such as the NKVD and KGB in Russia during and prior to the Stalinist era.

For many years the much vaunted Federal Bureau of Investigation (FBI) under J. Edgar Hoover devoted much more of its energies to compiling internal dossiers on the activities of American citizens than it did to fighting organised crime.)

In his summing up at the trial of Mary Barnes and Charlotte Barnacle in 1842, Mr Justice Patterson first expressed annoyance that the women had been questioned 'by a posse of police', and then demanded of the arresting officer whether or not he personally had questioned the accused. When assured by the man that he had not, his lordship congratulated him, saying that, 'he was glad to hear it. . . It was not the duty of a policeman to do so and he hoped he should not hear of it again.' In relation to the same crime, at the inquest on the victim, the coroner, touching with some apprehension on the alleged confessions made by the two accused women, declared:

> We have been told on credible authority that on the day they were apprehended, both made confessions to a Constable, admitting their guilt to the fullest extent. We always look with much disgust on such declarations of this kind, and there is generally a degree of sympathy for the parties when guilt is proved by conversations with a policeman or a turnkey. It savours too much of the French system for an English taste.

It was against this background of ignorance and prejudice that after its inception in 1836, the Leicester Borough Police Force began an uphill battle to bring law and order to the town and to persuade those responsible for local government that one of the roles of its officers was the investigation of crime.

One difficulty from the outset was that, in common with all of the other forces being established across the country, the management of the police devolved upon the Watch Committee, which was comprised primarily of hard-headed businessmen. As such, a rule of thumb was quickly implemented that a crime would continue to be investigated only so long as the culprit remained within the force area. If a suspect were to be identified as having moved outside of the borough, then further enquiries would only be made if the complainant was prepared to pay for the expenses incurred in continuance of the enquiry.

It was not until 1847 that, with a public acceptance of the presence of a police force in the town, it was possible to form any sort of detective department. The first reference is in February of that year when the Watch Committee notes contain a minute that; 'the two Sergeants of the Detective Police Force have silver badges.'

The officers referred to were Sergeants Thomas Haynes, who joined the force in 1838, and Francis Smith, both of whom in 1858 were promoted to the rank of Inspector.

As time progressed, so the department gradually expanded and officers of the rank of Constable were admitted. Soon after the turn of the century, the rank of Detective Superintendent first makes an appearance as Head of the

Detective Department, and seemingly by default, the assistant to the Head Constable. (It was not until 1915 that the term Chief Constable was used in the Borough, although both in Leicestershire and elsewhere the senior officers in county forces were referred to as Chief Constable.) In the Leicester Borough the first such reference was in 1906 to Detective Superintendent Herbert Allen who, upon the retirement of John Hall-Dalwood at the beginning of 1913, became Head Constable.

Resources were at this time still very limited. Photography as a science was well established; however, its practical applications in relation to police work were limited. Following the famous Houndsditch murders in 1910 which led to the Siege of Sidney Street, in order to take a post-mortem photograph of the body of one of the murdered officers, Sergeant Bentley, the body was dressed in his greatcoat and strapped to a stretcher – which was then propped up against a wall – and his helmet was firmly fixed on his head. The resulting image was, to say the least, macabre.

During the investigation in 1912 into the murder of Annie Jennings, which took place in her room in Archdeacon Lane, Sergeant Hart told the Coroner's Court that due to poor lighting, he could not take a photograph and instead produced a hand-drawn sketch.

Although photographs were obtained from the early years of the twentieth century, it was not until 1932 that the Leicester City Police Force established a proper Studio (Scenes of Crime) Department. In June of that year, Detective Constable Eric Pym was sent away to Wakefield in Yorkshire to attend a photograph and fingerprint course. On his return, the princely sum of £13 15s was spent on a Kodak camera and two stands, along with developing equipment.

One of the earliest logistical problems to be addressed by both the police and the local authority was what to do with the bodies of those unfortunates whose remains could not be disposed of until after the due processes of law had been completed. This of course applied not just to murder victims; anyone who had met a violent or unusual end could not be decently buried until a coroner's hearing had been convened. This difficulty was not merely one of accommodation, which was the least problematic. The most difficult issue in the days prior to refrigeration was the actual preservation of the cadaver.

Following the opening of the New Town Hall as the headquarters for the Police and the Fire Brigade in 1876, reference is made in March 1893 to the new mortuary building and the appointment of a 'keeper'. This building appears to have been situated at the rear of the town hall near to the drill yard and in close proximity to the Head Constable's living quarters. That the arrangement was most unsatisfactory is evidenced during the summer of that year when the presence in the mortuary room of the body of a woman who had been found dead in a house in Oxford Street was the cause of a spate of complaints from staff working in the building. John Watkinson, the chief clerk wrote:

. . . the stench from her corpse was of such a sickening nature that it made me unwell for several days, and upon two occasions since that time when men have been killed on the railway, the smell issuing from their mutilated remains has made me feel sick every time I passed through the yard to my office . . .

The matter was not properly addressed for some considerable time – in fact, until 1923 (although in the interim period, conditions were addressed). At one point in 1903, Dr C. Killick Millard suggested that the authorities might wish to consider a device which he had encountered in London:

I have ascertained at Battersea where a new mortuary has recently been erected [that] they have an iron tank on wheels, about the size and shape of a coffin, fitted with an airtight lid. A portion of this lid is glazed so that bodies can be identified without disturbing them. The tank is filled with a solution of formalin – the lid of which is heavy [and] is raised by a chain and counter poise.

Such an arrangement must be desirable where decomposed bodies have frequently to be dealt with, especially in hot weather. In Battersea a considerable number of bodies are recovered from the Thames – It is a question for your Committee to decide whether there would be a sufficient use to justify a similar provision in Leicester. – I am informed by the Chief Constable that during the present year, (10 months), only four bodies have been brought to the mortuary in a decomposed state. Last year the number was only two.

In 1923, a temporary mortuary was established at Lansdowne Road in the branch fire station which remained in use until 1927, when a brick-built facility was made available on Welford Road near to the cattle market gates. In 1960, it was once more re-sited to its present location at the Leicester Royal Infirmary.

The science of fingerprinting, which is central to the detection of crime, has been recognised since ancient times. One of the first specific references to the unique nature of prints was by Marcello Malpighi, a professor at Bologna University in 1686. In a treatise that he wrote on the subject, he discussed the ridges, spirals and loops that are present in an individual's prints, although he did not appear to make the link that these could be used to identify a person.

A similar discourse by John Evangelist Purkinje, a professor of anatomy at Breslau University in 1823, referred to his identifying nine fingerprint patterns, but again, he did not appreciate the implied potential. By the middle 1800s, interest in the subject was beginning to grow and Sir William Herschel, chief magistrate of the Jungipoor District of India, made a collection of people's prints (which he used in the signing of contracts), with the specific intention of being able to identify the person at a later time, thus for the first time making a practical use of fingerprints.

In 1882, Alphonse Bertillon, a clerk at the Préfecture of Police in Paris (who later became chief of the Department of Judicial Identity), instituted what became the Bertillon System of Anthropometry. This, although very flawed, used various measurements of a suspect's body (head size, arm length, etc.), and fingerprints to establish identities.

It was Sir Francis Galton, a British anthropologist and cousin of Charles Darwin, who in the late 1880s made one of the most significant discoveries. Galton was interested in hereditary factors and quickly eliminated fingerprints as being indicative of genetic links. What he did realise, however, was that a person's fingerprints do not change throughout their lives. He also classified the characteristics by which fingerprints can be identified, which today are known as 'Galton's Details'.

Meanwhile, under the direction of Sir Edward Richard Henry in India, the Calcutta Fingerprint Bureau was opened, using what became known as the Henry Classification System. Immediately after the turn of the twentieth century, New Scotland Yard, discontinuing the Bertillon System which was considered (correctly) to be unreliable, implemented Henry's Classification System, and in July 1901 the first fingerprint department was opened by the London Metropolitan Police.

There is only one drawback with a fingerprint system. It is reliant upon a known database for unidentified samples to be checked against. While at the beginning of the twentieth century the skills were available to obtain and read fingerprints, the appropriate databases with which to compare them did not exist and would not be in place for many years to come.

The other forensic tool that again did not become available to police until well into the twentieth century was the ability of forensic scientists to identify different blood groups. In 1901, Austrian Karl Landsteiner discovered that not all human blood was of the same composition, but it was to be another eight years (1909) before he was able to classify the constituents into specific groups. The purpose of Landsteiner's research was originally to resolve a common problem at the time: people dying after being given blood transfusions (which occurred unwittingly, as he found, due to a mixing of the wrong blood groups). Again, the potential of this knowledge in criminal investigations was not immediately apparent.

As the twentieth century progressed, so did the strength and experience of the Leicester Detective Department, though the days of modern technology and improved communications were still around the corner. The two-way radio system, for instance, did not come into use until the mid-1960s, and then, being dependant on signal strengths and location, it was not an efficient tool until some time after that. While the Borough Police had telephone links between the central and branch police stations as early as 1893 (with the Central Station at the Town Hall additionally being connected to 'the national system'), it was not until February 1947 that, in common with the rest of the country, the Leicester emergency services – police, fire and ambulance – could be contacted by the public through the '999' system.

During the 1960s, a new strategy in the fight against major crimes saw the setting up throughout the country of Force and Regional Crime Squads, dedicated to the pooling of resources in an attempt to effectively focus police investigations. This was to some degree facilitated in April 1967 by the enforced absorption of many Borough and City Forces into neighbouring County Forces, massively concentrating the manpower available.

What was perceived to be the ultimate step in the investigation of crime was the unravelling in the middle of the twentieth century of the mysteries of Deoxyribonucleic acid or DNA – the scientific makeup of the human body which can be linked to an organic forensic sample, such as blood or saliva, and can be allocated to an individual with almost pinpoint accuracy. The ensuing process of DNA fingerprinting, developed in 1985 by an English geneticist, Professor Sir Alec Jeffreys of Leicester University, has been used since then to solve many homicide cases worldwide and is now regarded, along with fingerprint evidence, as achieving as near a positive identification as is humanly possible.

The cases outlined in this book cover a period of 134 years, and in many of them the question that must be asked is if even one of these facilities had been available to the investigators of the time, just how much difference would have been made to the outcome?

# ACKNOWLEDGEMENTS

I would like to thank the following for their generosity in allowing me to include in this work photographs from their personal collections and archives: Edna Welford, for items from her late husband, Eric Rourke Welford's collection; Eric Selvidge; Geoff Fenn; Noel Haines; Leicestershire Constabulary. I would also like to thank County Archivist Carl Harrison and his staff at the Record Office for Leicestershire, Leicester and Rutland for access to and assistance in locating so many documents and other research items; the National Galleries of Justice, Nottingham; Ian Coutts for his tireless efforts in keeping my computer system functioning despite my best efforts to thwart him; and to John (Jock) Coutts for his first-hand knowledge concerning the investigation of the murder of William Johnstone. To each of these people and to any others who I may have inadvertently missed, I extend my most sincere thanks.

Unless otherwise stated, all other pictures are from the author's own collection.

# 1

# THE LAST MAN IN ENGLAND TO BE GIBBETED

## *James Cook, 1832*

It is our distressing task to exhibit to the public one of the most extraordinary facts that ever disgraced the criminal annals of any civilised country in the known world. The fact of which we speak is MURDER attended by circumstances of the most diabolical and barbarous nature such as the wildest and most fanciful imagination could scarce have dreamed of. In the heart of our town and close to our own firesides, it has had like a piece of ordnance, the effect of paralysing the thoughts and wholly occupying the minds of every individual within the reach of the report . . .

So began the article in the *Leicester Journal* of Friday 8 June 1832, which described the brutal murder by James Cook of John Paas at Cook's workshop in the busy town centre of Leicester ten days earlier on Wednesday 30 May 1832. The killing is particularly worthy of note, not merely for the horrific circumstances which accompanied it, but for other attendant factors.

In the final days of the Georgian era, this was the last crime of any great significance to be resolved in Leicester prior to the establishment of a Borough Police Force. The pursuance of Cook by the head constable, in his headlong flight to Liverpool in an attempt to take ship to America, along with his subsequent apprehension – taken from a rowing boat in the dawn light after a fierce sea chase, befitted the most imaginative of Victorian melodramas. Mystery was to continue to surround much of what happened in the hours following the murder, prior to Cook making his getaway – a mystery which his final confession, rife with lies and half truths, did little to resolve.

At forty-nine years of age, the victim John Paas was a partner in the firm of Messrs Paas & Co., Engravers of High Holborn, London. He was by profession a bookbinder's tool cutter, engraver and stationer, and one of his functions was to act as a commercial traveller for the company, visiting clients up and down the country, taking orders and collecting money for goods that had been supplied.

## Dreadful Murder of Mr. John Paas,
### OF 44, HIGH HOLBORN, LONDON.
*SKETCH OF THE ASSASSIN, JAMES COOK.*

In March 1832, bidding his wife farewell, Paas left his home at 44 High Holborn to set off on a round of visits that would take him well into the summer to complete. When he arrived at Leicester on the evening of Tuesday 29 May and booked in at the Stag and Pheasant in Humberstone Gate, John Paas had been on the road for two and a half months, and had collected some £50, a respectable amount of money for the time, from customers he had visited en route. Although the licensee of the inn did not know his guest by name, he later identified him as being 'the gentleman with a portmanteau and writing desk', which he used after breakfast the following morning to write a letter before going out about his business.

That business was for him to visit several booksellers and bookbinders in the town, leaving samples with each and returning later to collect their orders. The first client upon whom Paas paid a call was Richard Tebbutt, who had a bookshop a short distance from the Stag and Pheasant in the Haymarket. Having left some samples with Tebbutt, the commercial traveller obtained from him directions to the workshop of James Cook, and duly set off in the direction of Wellington Street.

James Cook was expecting the visit, and had laid careful plans for what was now to take place. An ambitious young man in his early twenties, Cook had served as an apprentice to a man named Johnson, a bookbinder in Albion Street, until his employer had died the previous year. On Johnson's death, in September 1831, the young man rented a workshop over a cowshed in Wellington Street from John Sawbridge, a local milkman, and set up in his own right.

At this point, we encounter the first puzzling aspect in this case. Cook's business appears to have flourished from the outset, so he was not in any financial difficulty. A comment was made by Mrs Johnson to John Paas when he had visited her just hours prior to his death that, 'there had been no turnover of debts to Cook from her husband's business', indicating that the young man either bought the business from her, or simply took Johnson's customers and began trading on his own. The former is probably the case, as all of the tools in Cook's Wellington Street shop were marked 'Paas', and as he had not bought them from the manufacturer, they had most likely been transferred from his original place of work. The fact is, though, that Cook was very busy fulfilling orders – he already employed an apprentice – a fourteen-year-old boy named Charles 'Joe' Watkinson – and there is no mention of him owing money to either Mrs Johnson or anyone else.

That the murder of John Paas was premeditated is clear. Charles Watkinson later stated at the inquest that during the week prior to the event, his employer had brought into the workshop a cleaver and a saw, and on the Saturday (although it was early summer), a hundredweight of coal for the fire was delivered.

At ten o'clock on Wednesday morning, according to the young apprentice, a tall gentleman whom he had never seen before, dressed in black with grey whiskers and a reddish face, came in and said, 'Good morning Mr Cook,' to which Cook replied, 'Good morning Sir'. The gentleman then asked where Mrs Johnson lived, and was told, 'in Albion Street', by Cook, who then turned around to the lad and whispered, 'Joe, you may go home now – and stay until I fetch you.'

Watkinson's statement is significant in that it gives clear evidence of plans being laid prior to the murder. The first thing that struck him was that, 'when the gentleman came into the shop, Cook turned very pale', which made the youngster think he had come for money, and later when he got home he mentioned it to his mother. It is more likely that at this point the enormity of the moment hit Cook, and his loss of colour was due to the knowledge of what was later to be done.

It was something of a surprise to the boy to be sent home because in his own words, 'at that time we were exceedingly busy, having more work than we could get through . . .' However, in the course of the previous week, his master had promised him a holiday for two or three days, saying at the same time that he himself intended to go out of town. Thus the murderer ensured that he now had the premises to himself, and any subsequent absence could be explained by the boy.

*The workshop where the murder of John Paas took place, taken from a wood cut published in the* Leicester Journal.

The apprentice also made some other important observations. It was he who mentioned that in the last week, his master had brought a saw from home and a cleaver with which he chopped some sticks and afterwards sharpened on a stone in the shop. Also, a few days previously, he had fetched three pennyworth of laudanum from Mrs Lewitt's shop for his master, who said he wanted to try an experiment, and the bottle was hanging on a nail on the wall for two or three days after.

James Cook had a brother, Michael, who lived at Queniborough and often came to the Wellington Street shop in a gig to help out with work; in fact, a supply of hay was kept by his employer to feed his brother's pony. Charles Watkinson told the inquest that Michael Cook had visited the workshop on the Saturday prior to the murder, and that he and James had left in the gig to go to Queniborough. In view of the later certainty that Cook had assistance, if not in the actual killing of John Paas, then certainly with the disposal of his body, the purpose of this visit is open to conjecture.

After passing the time of day for about fifteen minutes, Paas left two invoices with Cook for items that he had purchased last September, whereupon Cook asked him to return later that afternoon when he would settle up with him. Paas asked once more where he could find Mrs Johnson, the widow of Cook's old employer, and being directed to Albion Street, he set off to pay his respects and collect his dues.

En route to see the widow, the traveller first crossed over into Bowling Green Street to make a visit to another bookbinder – Robert Fisher Plant. Arriving at his premises around half past ten, John Paas left some samples with Plant, saying that he would return for them 'after dinner, when he had been back to see Mr Cook again'. If Cook thought that by luring Paas back to his premises late in the day he was being clever, exactly the opposite was true – the victim was inadvertently laying a clear trail back to his intended killer.

John Paas was next seen at around four o'clock in the afternoon when he returned to Richard Tebbutt's bookshop in the Haymarket to secure his order. The order, however, was not ready, so he told Tebbutt that he would make his way back to Wellington Street.

It is apparent that whatever his intention, on leaving Tebbutt's premises in the Haymarket, John Paas changed his mind and returned to his lodgings, where he was seen by the landlord sometime between five and six o'clock standing in the gateway of the inn, talking with two or three other commercial travellers. After a while, he walked off along Gallowtree Gate. This was the last time that he was seen alive.

The events which followed, and the circumstances of the murder, can be pieced together; first from the confession that Cook made while awaiting trial, and secondly from the statements made at the inquest by neighbours.

When John Paas returned to the workshop in Wellington Street, he and Cook were alone. Cook paid his victim the 12s that he owed, and Paas bent over the workbench to make out a receipt for the money. There now follows a contradiction between the evidence and Cook's version of what happened.

During the subsequent search of the room by the authorities, the invoice in question was found with John Paas' initial 'J' followed by the first letter of his surname, 'P', spoiled by a sudden and involuntary line dashed across the paper, indicating that he was struck a violent blow while signing his name.

*John Paas' signature.*

Later, at the enquiry, Paas' brother-in-law attested that the deceased never signed with just his initials – always his full name. Cook, however, insisted in his confession that this was not what happened, that in fact, he struck him after he had signed the document, while Paas was looking at some bindings, and that a fight of sorts ensued before he finally struck the fatal blow with a press bar.

Cook's confession, which will be examined more fully later, was fraught with patent lies, of which this is undoubtedly one. John Paas was a fairly tall man, standing 5ft 9in, and although Cook was taller, at just over 6ft, he would certainly have taken his best opportunity to strike the deceased a fatal blow – which would have been while he was bent over, concentrating on signing the bill. The involuntary scrawl, as the victim's hand jerked, makes the conclusion inescapable.

With the murder committed, the killer now needed to dispose of the body as expeditiously as possible, and it was here that the weakness in his planning began the chain of events leading to his downfall.

At seven o'clock on Wednesday evening, on leaving the workshop, Cook spoke to Mary Sawbridge, his landlord's wife, in the yard of their premises (his shop adjoined the Sawbridge's home), and told her that he would be coming back later that night to work for three or four hours, as his boy was poorly and he had some work which needed to be finished by Saturday, and consequently, he had made a fire in the grate of the shop.

By this time, Cook was obviously already engaged in getting rid of some of the more easily disposable body parts by burning them, although to leave them unattended was, as he later discovered, a risky business.

It was three hours later when he returned, much to the annoyance of John Sawbridge, who had waited up for him in order to let him in through the gate to the entry which separated the workshop and Sawbridge's living quarters. Giving Cook the key to the gate, he told him to lock up when he left and push the key back under the gate.

From this point on, it is certain that James Cook was assisted in his grisly task, and the prime suspect is his brother Michael. About three o'clock the following morning, two men, one of whom answered Cook's description, were seen in Rutland Street carrying between them a box, which it was later speculated contained the larger part of the dead man's remains. This reported sighting is frustratingly vague – it was published in the *Leicester Journal*, but the source is not given. If it is correct, however, it is crucial.

The two main unresolved questions in this case are: who helped Cook to dispose of the greater part of the remains and what was done with them? Michael Cook had a pony and gig in which such a box could be spirited away, and the men were only minutes from the edge of town where the gig could be hidden in the fields that spread out from the edge of the cricket ground on Wharf Street; the area was also very close to Cook's home in

Wheat Street. Either way, it was a risky business. Assuming that during the night, under cover of darkness, Cook let his accomplice into the workshop and they then packed as much of the body, along with John Paas' clothing as possible into the box, which took them into the early hours – and at that time of the year, by 3 a.m., (although it was a dark wet night), there would have been little time left before daylight. They then had to take the box through the streets, where having stowed it in the gig, they parted company: Michael (if it was him), driving off to dispose of his cargo; James to return to Wellington Street and continue cleaning up.

That they were cutting it fine is evidenced by the fact that as John Sawbridge was going out of the dividing entry at half past four to do his early morning milking, he was surprised to see Cook in the window of his workshop. It is reasonable here to presume that Cook also saw him, and having just got back, he was very likely still wearing his outdoor coat, and became worried that he had been seen coming in at that hour. In an attempt to cover his tracks, a few hours later at eight o'clock, he made a point of bumping into Mrs Sawbridge and said, 'Good morning Mrs Sawbridge, this is my second coming – I have been wet through this morning and in changing my coat, left my key in my other coat pocket and then went back again for it.'

During the middle of the morning, he again saw his landlady in the yard when he borrowed a mop, saying that he needed it in order to clean up the workshop. It was later discovered that there were traces of a considerable amount of blood on the floor, an attempt at which had been made to mop up, though some of it had seeped through the floorboards into the corner of the cowshed beneath the shop.

The stress of the charnel-house in which he was working eventually began to tell on the killer, and at about four o'clock on Thursday afternoon, Cook came out for a breath of air, and, complaining to John Sawbridge that he was feeling sick, took a walk with him to London Road where Sawbridge did his afternoon milking. On their return, Cook went once more into the workshop for a short while and then emerged, and after locking up, walked into the Flying Horse public house which was next door. There he remained (outside in the bowling alley, where he could keep an eye on the stairway to his shop) drinking until about nine in the evening. It was noted that, unusually for him, he had a brown silk purse in his possession containing quite a large amount of money. He then returned to the shop once more for a few minutes, doubtless to stoke up the fire and to lay on it the remaining part of the corpse before finally securing the premises and going home.

An hour later, just before ten, Mary Sawbridge spotted the light of a huge fire in the workshop window and sparks flying up from the chimney which was on fire, and called her husband. John Sawbridge, fearing that the building was alight, summoned John Nokes, the licensee of the Flying Horse, along with John Timson, a neighbour, and two other men named Carnall and Sansome who were in the pub at the time. Together they broke down the workshop door and discovered a large fire burning in the grate with what appeared to be a chunk of meat smouldering in the middle. Extinguishing the fire, the flesh was pulled away, and the shocked neighbours began to speculate as to what was going on.

Thomas Wisdich, Nokes' apprentice, was sent to Wheat Street, where James Cook lived with his father, brother and sister, to fetch him. On his arrival, the door was opened by Cook's father, and when called, James came downstairs in his nightshirt. Having been told about the fire, he dressed quickly and seemed both angry and disturbed that the workshop door had been forced in order to extinguish the fire. For the first time, he now told what was to be an oft repeated story – that he had bought a dog from a man who should have delivered it to him last Saturday, but had failed to do so, and the flesh was some dog-meat that he had bought and was now trying to dispose of.

Back at Wellington Street, accompanied by his sister, he persisted in the story that the remnants were dog-meat, but those gathered were not satisfied, and at eleven o'clock, Thomas Measures, a town constable, was summoned from his house which was in Wellington Street, about a hundred yards from Cook's shop.

Measures, out of his depth, was unsure what to do, and John Nokes finally insisted that he take Cook into custody on a holding charge of creating a nuisance by setting his chimney on fire. Measures still prevaricated, and leaving the scene, decided to put the matter in the hands of a magistrate. First he tried unsuccessfully to wake up Alderman Rawson, who also lived nearby, and then he went to the home of the mayor, also without success.

Returning to Wellington Street, Measures now decided to take Cook back to his father's house, and accompanied by Timson and Carnall, took him to Wheat Street. There they found Cook's father, and his brother, Joseph.

Measures now made a cardinal error; vacillating and uncertain, he gave James Cook into his father's custody to present him before the magistrates in the morning.

The men now returned to Wellington Street from where Carnall took the 'meat' to his own house for safe keeping, and it being the early hours of the morning, the group dispersed.

At 8 a.m., in the cold light of day, Friday 1 June, with the arrival on the scene of the magistrate, Alderman Rawson, things took on a different complexion. A bloodstained cleaver, the bottom of a pair of trousers, and a pencil with the initial 'P' were quickly found, and two surgeons, Messrs Denton and Macauley, soon identified the 'meat' as part of a human torso. In a slightly macabre touch, Carnall, prior to the arrival of Alderman Rawson, had returned the charred flesh, and replaced it *in situ*.

The town's senior law advisor, the town clerk Thomas Burbidge, was now summoned and took charge of the situation.

### BRIGGS's COACH OFFICE,
*Hay Market, Leicester*

J. BRIGGS and SON beg gratefully to express their acknowledgement for the very distinguished patronage they have received in their Coaching Department, particularly to the Inhabitants of the Town of Leicester and Neighbourhood and, in submitting the annexed List of Coaches, trust still to merit the approbation and support of their Friends and the Public generally, assuring them that no exertion shall be wanting to render their conveyances as expeditious a degree of travelling as can be effected with safety, regularity, comfort and accommodation.

VIVIAN a new and only direct Coach to Cheltenham (without change of Coach or Coachman) every morning at a quarter before seven (Sundays excepted)

CORRECTED LIST OF
## *ROYAL MAILS AND POST COACHES*
FROM THE
## *GEORGE HOTEL, LEICESTER*

| Miles. | MORNING. | Time. |
|---|---|---|
| 18 | Ashby-de-la-Zouch ROYAL MAIL | hf past 6 |
| 27 | Burton-upon-Trent ROYAL MAIL .. | ditto |
| 92 | Barton water -Side .. | ditto |
| 36 | Bingham ........ | ditto 6 |
| 48 | Banbury ............. | 8 |
| 204 | Carlisle DEFIANCE ... | 6 |
| 27 | Derby................. | 6 |
| 72 | Doncaster..... | half-past 6 |
| 66 | Gainsborough ...... | ditto |
| 92 | Huddersfield .......... | 4 |
| 190 | Halifax ............... | 4 |
| 98 | London DEFIANCE through Northampton | 5 |
| 98 | London TIMES, hf-past 10 | |
| 101 | Leeds EXPRESS .. | ditto 4 |
| 60 | Lincoln .......... | ditto 6 |
| 38 | Leamington ....... | ditto 8 |
| 14 | Lutterworth ........ | 8 |
| 134 | Manchester DEFIANCE | 6 |
| 72 | Macclesfield .......... | 6 |
| 32 | Northampton Coaches | 5 &10 |
| 26 | Nottingham EXPRESS .. | 4 |
| 26 | Ditto  COMMERCIAL | 5 |
| 26 | Ditto  LARK...... | 7 |
| 46 | Newark .............. | 7 |
| 74 | Oxford REGULATOR | 8 |

| Miles. | MORNING. | Time. |
|---|---|---|
| 21 | Rugby ............... | 8 |
| 64 | Sheffield ............. | 4 |
| 38 | Warwick............. | 8 |
| 62 | Woodstock ........... | 8 |
| 298 | Edinburgh Express .... | 4 |
| 44 | Birmingham CRITERION | 11 |
| 27 | Coventry ............ | 11 |
| 38 | Leamington ......... | 11 |
| 38 | Warwick .............. | 11 |
| | **AFTERNOON** | |
| 18 | Ashby-de-la-Zouch ..... | 10 |
| 26 | Burton-upon-Trent ..... | 10 |
| 26 | Derby TIMES .......... | 6 |
| 98 | London,COMMERCIAL | 8 |
| 98 | London EXPRESS ...... | 10 |
| 94 | London RED ROVER through Welford | 10 |
| 112 | Liverpool RED ROVER through Staffordshire Potteries ........... | 10 |
| 18 | Melton OMNIBUS ...... | 7 |
| 86 | Manchester ........... | 10 |
| 26 | Nottingham HARK FOR-WARD | |
| 26 | Nottingham TIMES ...... | 6 |
| 32 | NorthamptonCoaches | 8 &10 |
| 11 | Loughborough ACCOM-MODATION ......... | 5 |

☞ *Parcels and Luggage conveyed daily, to every City and Manufacturing Town in the Kingdom.*
### PERFORMED BY J. BRIGGS & SON

Neat Post Chaises, Hearse and Mourning Coaches, Coach and Landau Flys, on the most reasonable terms, with good Horses and careful Drivers.

*Having been left in the custody of his father, Cook made his way (probably assisted by his brother) to Loughborough where he picked up the early morning coach to Liverpool.*

Not unexpectedly, James Cook had already absconded, and a report was soon received that a man aged about twenty-two, with large whiskers and a long face, wearing a blue coat and brown trousers, with a green and white handkerchief, had boarded the early morning 'Defiance Coach' from Loughborough around 6.30 a.m., bound for Manchester and Liverpool. While waiting for the coach at Loughborough, the young man had attempted to sell various items, including a watch and gold pin, which were later identified as belonging to John Paas.

Thomas Burbidge immediately set about apprehending Cook and putting the murder enquiry on a proper footing. First he despatched the town's head constable, George Owston (not to be confused with the later office of Head Constable of the Borough Police Force), along with one of the town's constables, a man named Cummins, who knew Cook and could identify him, on the Red Rover Coach to Liverpool with a brief to bring Cook back.

Next, he addressed the fact that if Cook had burned some of the body parts, he had also made alternative provision for those which would not burn, along with the victim's missing clothing. An immediate search was ordered of all cesspits and other likely places within a five mile radius. Finally, he sat down to write to John Paas' partners in London, apprising them of what had taken place and asking for relatives to come to Leicester in order that an inquest could be convened.

The search for the missing body parts was unsuccessful, and it was now to become a matter of concern as to what Cook had done with them – a question that was never answered. Equally of consequence were the circumstances of the killer being allowed – and assisted – to escape. He could not have gone without the connivance of his father, into whose custody the unfortunate Measures had handed him. (Thomas Measures was severely castigated at the inquest for his shortcomings; however, it must be remembered that this was in the days before a police force had been instituted. Measures would, in reality, have been little more than a glorified watchman whose main function was to act as a town servant, waiting on at civic banquets – of which there were many.) It was already around midnight when the constable and his companions left the house in Wheat Street. For Cook to then walk from Leicester to Loughborough, a distance in excess of 12 miles, and at six o'clock the same morning to be selling items of the dead man's property while waiting to board the coach, would have required a considerable feat of stamina. Also, the description of him makes no reference to his being travel-stained or weary, as he inevitably would have been. It is far more likely that once more, Michael Cook was somewhere in the background, waiting to provide transport.

Thomas Burbidge, not about to compound the errors already committed, had the entire family arrested and locked up in the town gaol while he awaited the detention of the main suspect. Among other things, he also created an incentive for anyone with knowledge of the murderer's whereabouts to hand him over by arranging for a reward of £200, half from the Home Office and half from the victim's partners, to be paid on his apprehension and conviction; a very substantial sum for the time.

George Owston proved himself an able investigator, and with the assistance of his counterpart in Liverpool, over the weekend quickly set about finding his man.

It was not long before the local constables came up with information that a stranger using the name of Perry had arranged to board the *Carle of Calton*, a ship standing 5 miles off of Liverpool under the Black Rock, which was to sail with the 3.a.m. tide on Tuesday morning. Cummins, accompanied by one of the Liverpool constables and some local river men, all of whom were promised a substantial reward if the murderer was taken prisoner, laid wait in the dark through the early hours of Tuesday morning for the boat rowing the passenger out to the *Carle of Calton*. Their patience was rewarded at about 2.30 a.m. by the sight of a dinghy manned by two watermen, with James Cook (identified by Cummins) sitting on the side. A desperate chase ensued, with the rowing boat, after attempting to outrun its pursuers, turning about in an effort to regain the shore, and finally intercepted in the shallows where Cook, jumping from the boat, was brought down in the surf by one of Cummins' men. Having subdued Cook, who in a last effort to evade his fate attempted to swallow a bottle of laudanum which he was carrying (probably the same one that he had sent young Joe Watkinson out to buy), he was searched and found to be in possession of 41 sovereigns, 7 half sovereigns and a guinea – the remainder of the proceeds of his crime.

Cook was taken before the Liverpool magistrates later that morning for formal identification and then handed into the custody of George Owston for escort to Leicester.

Once the killer was safely in the town gaol (and by coincidence, the gaol keeper was the father of George Owston), Thomas Burbidge began a series of interviews with him to prepare the case for trial at the next Assizes.

The most vexing question that Burbidge needed to address was, how were the majority of the victim's remains disposed of? The suspicion in Thomas Burbidge's mind that Cook was not alone in the commission of the murder had, by now, become a certainty.

Asked to explain what he had done, Cook told his interviewer that he had cut the body into small pieces and burned them during Wednesday night through into the early hours of Thursday, and in fact, after sending his apprentice away, he had bought in another hundredweight of coal to ensure that there was sufficient fuel for the purpose. Burbidge made the point that according to the surgeons involved in the investigation, it would have been impossible to have destroyed organs such as the lungs, to which the prisoner replied in a melancholy tone, 'Ah Sir, they never tried the experiment'.

Next, Burbidge put it to him that burning the intestines would have created a stench which would have alerted the entire neighbourhood. The answer he received was equally evasive, '. . . I know nothing about that Sir, it was a very stormy night and a great deal of rain fell, perhaps these may account for it.'

The answers were a patently obvious tissue of lies and the town clerk now went on to the subject of the victim's bones. How, he asked, was it possible that no remains of John Paas' bones or skull were found? To this, Cook replied that they had burned so well that, placing the fingers of his right hand upon the palm of his left, he said, 'I could smash them thus'. He did, however, concede that some bones found nearby on a dung heap could have been from his victim.

One of the killer's answers does, however, give a small clue as to the possible exclusion of his father from involvement in the murder and subsequent disposal of the body – though not in facilitating his escape. James Cook's father had told the examining magistrates that during Wednesday night, anxious by his son's absence from the house, he had dressed and gone to the workshop, where he had knocked, but receiving no answer, returned home. The prisoner stated that he was in the back yard at the time and, recognising his father's footsteps (and doubtless his voice), he had refused to let him in for fear of discovery.

No witness had seen the elder Cook in Wellington Street, and if he were a part of the murder he would never have drawn attention to himself in this way, so it can be presumed that he was telling the truth and arrived unexpectedly while James and his accomplice were preparing the body parts for removal.

Although this tends to eliminate Cook Senior from the early stages of the crime, it does raise the question of why, if James sometimes worked all night, was the older man sufficiently suspicious on this occasion to get up in the early hours of the morning and go to his son's place of work? Is it possible that he suspected James and Michael were up to something nefarious and he wanted 'a cut' of the proceeds?

As to the question of why, when the greater part of his grisly task had been accomplished on Thursday night, the murderer set such a huge fire and put the last piece of flesh on it (the body part was in the region of 30lbs in weight) before going home, his reply again does not ring true. He told Burbidge that in his then state of mind, he did not care whether he was apprehended or not.

Given the degree of premeditation involved in the murder, it is possible that this was, in fact, the last part of the scheme to destroy all traces of the event. Thomas Burbidge put it to Cook that the level of the fire that he set was such that it was bound to be discovered. Within a very short time it had set the chimney on fire and sparks were flying upwards for all to see.

A reasonable supposition is that the murderer's intention – having left the last piece of evidence to be consumed – was in reality to set fire to the entire building. A proven callous killer with no regard for human life, and the fact of the fire-fighting facilities in the borough being minimal, the conflagration would also have destroyed all of the adjacent properties, which would have been to his advantage. There is no doubt that when brought from his bed by Thomas Wisdich, Cook was anticipating being told that his workshop had burnt down.

The town clerk did not believe a word the murderer said and flatly put it to him that he was lying, and demanded to know who had assisted him after the murder. Cook, once more with complete disdain for the evidence, solemnly declared that '. . . no person but himself knew. . . and that every other person was as innocent as a lamb. . .'

In the remaining days before his trial, the prisoner occupied himself by continually reading religious tracts and singing hymns. His oft repeated words of repentance must be treated with a high degree of scepticism in view of the fact that he persisted until the very end in refusing to identify his accomplice. On the evening of 9 June, the magistrates convened at the gaol and released from custody Cook's father, his sister and his brother Joseph. At this juncture, Michael, the prime suspect, was kept in custody; however, with no evidence forthcoming against him, he also was later released.

On Saturday 28 July, eleven days before the date set for his trial, Cook announced to one of his gaolers, a man named Richards, that he wished to 'unburden his mind', and asked to see the town clerk, who arrived around one o'clock in the afternoon.

The following is the verbatim record, made by Burbidge, of the interview.

*Burbidge*: Cook, first let me ask you, was the murder premeditated?
*Cook*: It was Sir.
*Burbidge*: When did it first enter your mind? Was it when you sent the last order for goods, and enquired when Mr Paas might be expected in Leicester?
*Cook*: No Sir. I never did enquire that, and I never thought of the crime until I received the invoice of those goods and the letter stating when Mr Paas would be at Leicester, and I then determined to commit the deed.

Burbidge then asked about his motive for the crime, to which the prisoner replied that it was to possess himself of money and better his position.

*Burbidge*: How did you accomplish it – did you strike him while he was writing the receipt – or how was it?
*Cook*: No Sir, he had written the receipt. [The evidence of the spoiled signature would indicate that the killer is lying here, possibly to make his position look better, in that his victim died in an ensuing struggle.]
*Burbidge*: What did you strike him with and whereabouts?
*Cook*: I struck him with the press bar on the back of the head.

*Burbidge:* If he was not writing, how did you get the opportunity?

*Cook:* I got behind him when he was looking at some bindings and other things.

*Burbidge:* How came you to let the opportunity pass, was it that your mind misgave you, or did you at all change your mind?

*Cook:* My mind misgave me many times, and I was very near indeed to letting him go without striking him at all, but at last Satan prevailed with me and I struck him the blow.

*Burbidge*: Did that one blow kill him?

*Cook:* No Sir, he did not fall then. He cried out 'Murder!' and actually opened the shop door and seized the heavy hammer and came towards me, and I thought at that moment to myself that he would have killed me, or at least that I should be instantly discovered, and I fully expected it, but I had bought the laudanum to provide myself for any event of that kind. However, he dropped the hammer as I supposed his strength failed him and I struck him again on the head, and he fell, and I then struck him two or three times more, but he never spoke or stirred afterwards.

After being further questioned by the town clerk concerning his motives and the crucial matter of the disposal of the body parts, Cook's final declaration to him was, 'Oh Sir, if I had not gone drinking after the deed, but had begun my work two hours sooner than I did, every piece of the body and all belonging to him would have been destroyed, and all human detection have become impossible, but', he added, 'thank God I was detected. I should have gone on in wickedness, and I am sure I should have destroyed myself also very soon.'

The confession was sufficient to send Cook to the gallows. On the morning of Wednesday 8 August 1832, after a short hearing of the evidence, the judge sentenced him to be executed by hanging and his body afterwards hung in chains – a penalty reserved for only the most brutal of crimes.

In a final twist of irony, the seal affixed by the Assize Court to the indictment against James Cook had been engraved by his victim John Paas, and bore his name.

By ten o'clock on Friday 10 August, a crowd estimated at 40,000 had gathered outside the County Gaol on Welford Road awaiting the appearance of the murderer for his public execution. In a final effort to elicit the truth, Mr Denton, the attorney for the victim's relatives, interviewed Cook in his cell in an endeavour to find out what had been done with John Paas' remains. To the very end Cook denied the existence of an accomplice and persisted in his story that everything was burned.

Following his execution, the body of James Cook was put into a specially made metal cage and hung up on a gibbet, erected on the outskirts of the town in Saffron Lane on the road leading from the Aylestone toll gate to Countesthorpe (this later became the junction of Saffron Lane and Aylestone Road).

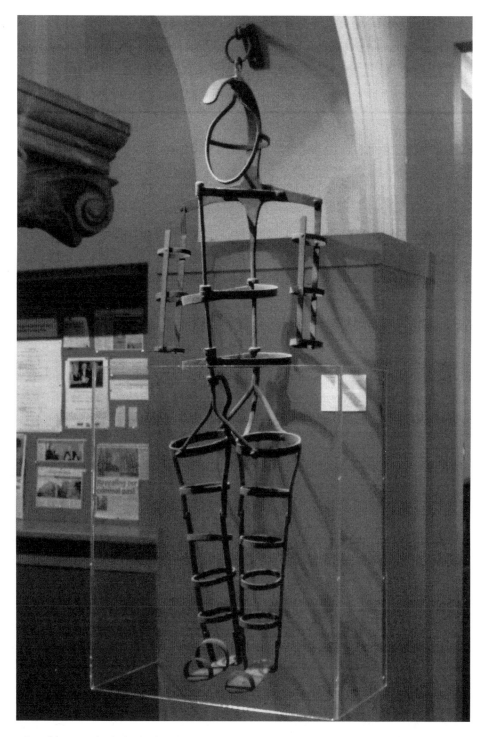

*The gibbet in which the body of James Cook was displayed was, for many years, exhibited at the Guildhall Museum in Leicester before being removed to the National Galleries of Justice at Nottingham. (Courtesy National Galleries of Justice)*

Such was the notoriety of the event that great crowds flocked to view the gibbet, and fearing public disorder, after three days and an outcry by some of the town's leading citizens, the Home Office instructed that the body be taken down and the gibbet dismantled.

James Cook was, in fact, the last executed murderer in England to be displayed in this manner. Before the end of the year, the practice was abolished by parliament.

Although Michael Cook was the prime suspect as his brother's accomplice, nothing was ever proved. In the absence of any other evidence, it has to be assumed that the motive for John Paas' murder was, as he stated, simply robbery, and that while the sum taken from him was a little over £50 – a great deal of money for the time – it was hardly sufficient for the immense risks taken and the brutality involved.

For all of Cook's preparations, the crime was a botched affair. A clear trail was laid by the victim to the workshop where he met his death. The majority of the body parts and Paas' clothing were efficiently disposed of, but at the end in the final stage, a fire intended to complete the job was bungled. Having absconded during the night, the murderer then signalled his destination when boarding the Liverpool coach at Loughborough by attempting to sell some of his victim's possessions.

As a postscript, it is worth noting that Cook's nemesis, Thomas Burbidge, was himself a shadowy and dishonest figure. Prior to the passing of the Municipal Reform Act three years later in 1835, the administration of the borough's affairs was highly suspect, with members of the Corporation lining their own pockets through illict land deals and mismanagement of borough funds at every possible opportunity, all of which were orchestrated by the town clerk.

In January 1836, under the terms of the new Act, a fresh and highly respectable council was voted into office; their first actions were to create a Borough Police Force and dismiss Burbidge from office. Over the next twenty years, prior to his death in 1855 in a debtors' prison, he spent most of his time and efforts suing the council for large sums of non-existent money which he alleged were owed to him.

# 2

# AS MUCH AS WOULD LIE ON A SHILLING

*Mary Barnes & Charlotte Barnacle, 1842*

In the spring of 1842 the borough of Leicester, typical of many other Midlands towns, was a less than salubrious place in which to live. Its 60,000 occupants were, for the most part, housed in overcrowded terraced dwellings, often six to a room, with no running water or sanitation. A large part of the population relied for their meagre income on the precarious cottage industry of framework knitting, which was based on rented frames in the workers home, and yielded barely a sufficient return to allow the operatives to eke out a living. Disease was endemic, and with the town's primary water supply – the River Soar – polluted with refuse and sewage, annual attacks of a particularly virulent 'summer diarrhoea' resulted in an infant mortality rate which was well above the national average. Overlaying this dismal picture of poverty and depression were the added factors that the town was rife with the activities of the Chartist Movement, led by Thomas Cooper, a journalist who had a shop in Churchgate, and the first of the massive influx of Irish immigrants which was filling the lodging houses and rookeries of Abbey Street and Belgrave Gate.

Typical of this situation were the noxious overcrowded stews and hovels of the Oxford Street and Southgates district. This was one of the poorest districts of the town. Houses were not numbered (thus it is not possible now to locate exactly the Barnes' dwelling), and the area was a maze of alleys and courtyards known only by their local names. Every household shared a water pump and communal dry ash privy with probably four or six others. In 1840, the borough's newly-appointed Nuisance Inspector, George Bown, made early comment on the 'accumulated filth in every corner of the town and the abundance of slaughter houses, pigsties [kept as a hedge against starvation] and privies, all within a few feet of overcrowded dwellings.'

The Barnes family; Stephen, a framework knitter and his wife, Ann, with their eighteen-year-old daughter Mary, and fifteen-year-old son Isaac, moved into one of the houses fronting onto Oxford Street at the beginning of March 1842. Stephen rented the house because it had an upper storey in which he could install his knitting frame, and had the additional bonus that it came with two sitting tenants, seventy-year-old Mary Waring, who lived in the garret, and an older woman, Susan Mee, known simply as 'Old Sukey' who rented a room – both of whom would be sub-letting from him.

As was the custom, the Barnes, soon after moving in, found for themselves another lodger, a nineteen-year-old girl by the name of Charlotte Barnacle, who, until recently, had lived in the district with her aunt. On their taking over the house, Mary Waring negotiated with the Barnes a move from her garret to a room on the ground floor at the back of the house, and on 2 April Charlotte moved in with her, the arrangement being that they should share the room and sleep together. It is most likely that Barnacle was in practice Mary Waring's tenant and shared her sub-let status.

Mary Waring quickly had reason to question the wisdom of taking on her new companion. The day after Charlotte moved in, on Sunday 3 April, soon after breakfast, a 'gentleman friend', Joe Sanders, arrived and stayed with the young woman until around lunchtime. Mary Waring was not pleased and after Sanders left, hard words ensued between the old lady and the young woman.

It is from this point on that the story of the plot by Charlotte Barnacle and Mary Barnes begins to unfold. The question is: what was the true nature of that plot, and what was the motivation behind it?

About twelve noon the following Wednesday, both of the young women went to see a neighbour, Ann Johnson, a widow who lived nearby in Jones' Yard, one of the courts off of Grange Lane. Barnes asked of her, 'Mrs Johnson, what sort of stuff is poison?' To justify the enquiry, the girls passed the question off by saying that they had been discussing the suicide three years ago of a local woman named Catherine Smith who had poisoned herself. Mrs Johnson told them that the most common poison – arsenic – was a powder, rather like flour, and that *as much as would lie on a shilling* would kill someone.

It was at this early stage that the pair told their first calculated lie. Barnacle mentioned that 'Old Sukey', who also lodged with them, had been asking for some arsenic to destroy bugs. Mary's father, she said, had been to a shop to get some, but they would not let him have it by himself, and he, along with his wife and another daughter (Sarah, who no longer lived with them) had then gone together and procured it. This, Stephen Barnes later testified, was totally untrue, and as events developed, was quite a significant comment. Unfortunately, when the case came to trial, the prosecution completely missed the implications of this fabrication.

About an hour later, Mary and Charlotte returned to the Barnes' house, where, having spoken to Mary's younger brother, Isaac, both went into the room shared by the older girl and Mary Waring, who was away from the house at the nearby workshop of Mark Weston where she was employed as a winder.

*To the left of the Swan & Rushes public house runs Grange Lane (also known in the nineteenth century as Green's Lane) and to the right is Oxford Street. Both nowadays bear little resemblance to the slum area of 1842. As part of the city council's post-war redevelopment schemes during the 1950s and '60s, all of the old courtyards of the district were pulled down. The house where the murder of Mary Waring took place, along with Jones' Yard, would have been between the two streets, within a hundred yards of where the Swan & Rushes now stands.*

According to Isaac, they remained closeted away for most of the afternoon during which time, so far as he knew, Charlotte was teaching Mary how to bind shoes, which was her job. He remembered Charlotte Barnacle leaving the house for about a quarter of an hour, at around three o'clock, to walk up to Peacock Lane in order to take the work they had done to her employer.

Soon after Charlotte returned from Peacock Lane, the two young women went out together into the town centre, where they first visited a chemist's shop in Hotel Street owned by William Wales Stephens, and attempted to buy a pennyworth of arsenic. Mr Stephens refused to serve them on the grounds that he never supplied poisons to strangers.

Next they went to the nearby premises in the Market Place of another chemist, one Joseph Hooley Lockyer. There they once again asked for a pennyworth of arsenic. This time, less cautious than William Stephens, Lockyer, having enquired for what purpose they required the arsenic and told by Charlotte Barnacle that it was for 'bugs and fleas', agreed to let them make the purchase and went into the back of the shop, leaving his boy, Thomas Murdy, to deal with the sale. Having made a small parcel of the arsenic, Murdy began to make out a label which read, '*J.H. Lockyer, Chemist &c. – Arsenic – Poison – Market Place, Leicester*'. The girls, who both appeared to be in high spirits and were swearing a lot because neither of them could read or write, asked him what he was doing, and when he explained what was on the label, one of them said, 'you need not put it on'. Ignoring this, he continued to ensure that the deadly contents of the packet were clearly identified.

At 4.30 p.m. they returned to the house in Oxford Street, and while Mary Barnes had a cup of tea with her brother, Barnacle once more went to her own room. Just after 5 p.m., Mary Waring came in from work to take her tea break, and half an hour later, before returning to the Weston's frame shop, she filled a large tea kettle as was her custom, and left it on some bricks in the hearth in readiness for when she came back around nine o'clock that evening.

After Mary Waring returned to work at 5.30 p.m., no one saw Barnacle again until around 7.30 p.m., when she returned home, having presumed to have been to work at her employers in Peacock Lane. There was a back door out of the room she shared with Mary Waring, and it was quite easy for her to come and go without it being noticed by the other occupants of the house. Also, with the family being engaged upstairs in the framework knitting business, it would have been a simple matter for either her or Mary Barnes to have gone unseen into the empty parlour and tipped the contents of the arsenic packet into the tea kettle in the fire grate.

As the evening progressed, so events began to unfold. Eight o'clock found the two young women once more in the town centre attempting to buy a further supply of arsenic. They went this time to the shop belonging to Thomas William Palmer, a chemist in Market Street, where Barnacle, described by Mr Palmer as 'the elder of the two', asked for a pennyworth of arsenic, once again declaring that they wanted it for 'bugs and fleas'. Palmer refused to sell them the poison and they went away laughing loudly.

At the women's trial, Mr Hildyard for the Crown presented this visit to a third chemist as an aberration on Palmer's part, that he had got the time wrong and that the prisoners had visited all three chemists during the afternoon, being refused at two before succeeding with the third. This was actually a piece of gross incompetence on his part.

Thomas Palmer and his assistant, John Charles Burrell, were both positive that Barnacle and Barnes were in the shop together at eight o'clock in the evening. They described the clothing that they were wearing and the fact that neither wore a bonnet. In evidence, the chemist said, 'I am positive it was near eight o'clock. My assistant was in the shop, also Mr Collier, proprietor of the *Mercury*. When I saw them at the Station House [the next morning] I immediately recognised them as the persons who applied for the poison.' Had the prosecution taken notice of this evidence (Hildyard did not even bother to make an enquiry of Mr Collier who would have added further corroboration), the Crown could have gone a long way to answering at least one of the questions that has plagued later examination of this crime – what were the intentions of the two women?

On their return to Oxford Street, Barnacle went into the house while Barnes paid a fleeting visit a few doors away to Ann Johnson's in Jones' Yard. (The reason for this visit and the two women splitting up was never clarified, but the indication is that Barnes was now frightened and did not wish to go home with Barnacle.) It was at this point that a young apprentice chair maker, George Carnall, overheard a conversation that was probably one of the most crucial pieces of evidence in the entire case.

At a quarter past eight, Carnall went to enter Ann Johnson's front door when he bumped into Mary Barnes leaving. The couple obviously knew each other well because Barnes took the young man up the yard to where it was quiet and said to him, 'We've got something on foot, but I dare not tell you what.' Intrigued, George Carnall asked, 'Tell me what it is, let me be knowing.'

She replied, 'I dare not hardly,' but on his pressing her she added, 'I've bought some jalap and Barnacle has put it in the tea pot' – the lad was not positive later whether she had said 'tea pot' or 'tea kettle'. In explanation, the girl told him that the 'old lady' had offended both her and her lodger, and that the lodger had bought some jalap which she had put in her teapot 'to serve her out'.

It was at this point that Charlotte Barnacle came out of the Barnes' house and Carnall, on seeing her said, 'Why, that is Lot Barnacle', indicating that while he knew her, he had not realised she was the lodger in question.

Barnacle spotted her accomplice and shouted, 'Molly Barnes!', but Barnes slipped away up a nearby entry to hide herself.

Charlotte first went back into the house, and then returned moments later, and crossing over, demanded of Carnall, 'Have you seen her again?'

From her hiding place in the entry, Mary whispered to the lad, 'Say no.'

George Carnall, however, was having no part in whatever was going on and said, 'Yes, I've got her here,' revealing her hiding place.

Obviously annoyed, Barnacle said, 'Damn you Molly, they are having it, come, let us go!'

Panicking, Mary Barnes said, 'No I daren't go, for I am sure they will taste it, there will be something the matter.'

Angrily the other woman said, 'Oh be damned, they'll never taste it.'

Still trying to buy some time, the younger girl said, 'Stop while I go up the yard to fetch my work.' She then went off up the yard and, coming back a short while later, both women went into the Barnes' house. Carnall could not see whether she had brought any work back or not, and the likelihood is that she went off to compose herself.

The submission later made by the prosecution was that it was the intention of the two young women solely to poison Mary Waring as retribution for her having upset them in a domestic matter and things got out of hand.

From the conversation which George Carnall overheard (combined with the evidence of later events), this was clearly not the case – '. . . *they* are having

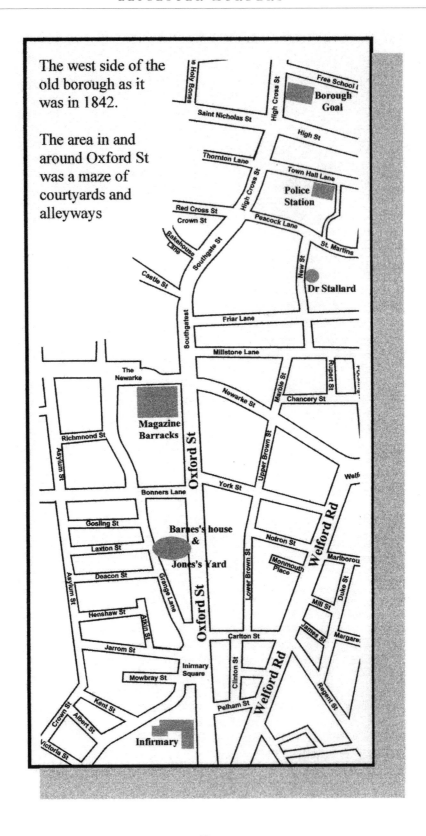

The west side of the old borough as it was in 1842.

The area in and around Oxford St was a maze of courtyards and alleyways

it. . .' / 'I daren't go, for I am sure *they* will taste it. . .' / 'be damned, *they'll* never taste it'. The references are clear – '*they*' can only refer to the members of the household, as opposed to '*her*' or '*she*' – meaning Mrs Waring. Apart from any other consideration, Waring was a creature of habit and she was not due in yet from work. The implication is plain; the intended victims were to include Mary Waring and any members of the Barnes family who drank from the poisoned tea kettle.

When Mary Waring returned from work at nine o'clock, she joined the two girls and Mary Barnes in the parlour in order to heat up the kettle, which by now contained sufficient arsenic to poison most of the street. While the kettle was on the fire boiling, Ann Barnes sent her daughter out to fetch some milk. Once it was boiled and Mrs Waring had filled her teapot from it, Charlotte Barnacle took herself off with the old lady to their room and remained with her while she drank some of the tea. Satisfied that her victim had consumed a quantity of the arsenic, she then once more left the house.

Fifteen minutes later, Mary Waring, the effects of the poison beginning to take effect, went back into the parlour and told Ann Barnes that she felt unwell. Mrs Barnes took her back into her own room where the old woman was taken violently ill with stomach pains and shaking, and she became wracked with sickness and diarrhoea. Ann Barnes then poured for herself some tea from the victim's pot, but finding it almost cold, only drank about half of the cupful before setting it aside, then, topping up the pot from the kettle, she gave the old woman a further drink in an attempt to ease her discomfort. The result was (not unexpectedly) exactly the opposite, and within a quarter of an hour, she was violently ill again.

The two girls now rejoined them and they got Waring onto her feet in an attempt to ease her pain. At this point, Stephen Barnes, obviously aware that something was going on, came down from his workshop on the top floor and found the group with Waring, who was standing by supporting herself on the bedstead. As the old woman refused to allow a doctor to be sent for, he returned back upstairs to continue working, while Barnacle went across the road to tell Ann Johnson that their lodger was seemingly very ill.

It was not long before Ann Barnes was also affected by the poison, and when her husband came back downstairs around eleven o'clock, he found her in the chimney corner being extremely ill. Having taken her to their bedroom, he said that he would go down and get her some tea. Stephen Barnes went back down to the parlour and got his own teapot, put some fresh tea in it and asked the girls, who were in the other room with the dying woman, if they had got any hot water. One of them replied that there was some in the kettle, but it needed some fresh water and she would top it up. He then went back upstairs to his wife who later recollected hearing the sound of water being pumped in the yard below.

On coming down again after a little while, Stephen Barnes remained a short time with the girls and Mary Waring while the kettle, which he noted was more than half full, boiled. He then took the teapot upstairs and, after it had stood a few minutes, poured a cup and gave it to his wife who drank part of it while he was with her, but the girls called him back down to Mrs Waring, as they said they dared not stay in the room with her on their own.

On his return to the room, he found the old woman lying on her back, mouth open, unable to speak. She remained in this condition until at 2 a.m. when she finally died. During this time, both of the young women remained in the room with him, and Mary, having fetched his teapot and replenished it from the kettle, gave him two cups from it, which he later said he drank gratefully, 'feeling so fatigued with work and running up and down stairs.' Barnacle also accepted a cup from the pot, took a sip and refused to drink any more saying that, 'it was not good'. Mary Barnes refused to touch the brew.

The implications here are damning – having filled up the kettle, both of the young women were completely aware that at this stage, having killed Mary Waring, they were now plying Stephen Barnes with the same deadly poison.

During this time, realising that Waring's death was imminent, Stephen called his wife to join them; however, on managing with difficulty to make her way to the room, Ann Barnes was too ill to do anything other than sit in a chair. After the old woman died, Barnes, now alarmed by his wife's deteriorating condition, decided to fetch a doctor and left the house to go to nearby New Street where Dr John Stallard lived. When later questioned, he said in evidence that his daughter and Barnacle, 'did not appear at all concerned at the state the deceased was in – after her death they went for some neighbours to lay her out'. (Between two and three o'clock that morning, both of the young women went across to wake Ann Johnson and ask her to return with them to help lay the body out. Johnson refused, whether due to the lateness of the hour, or because she suspected that something was amiss, is not known.)

On his arrival at Dr Stallard's house, Stephen Barnes managed to waken the household before himself being taken violently ill. When Stallard came down into the street, dressed and ready to go back to the house with him, he found Barnes hanging onto a lamppost vomiting. As they were making their way from New Street towards Oxford Street, the two men encountered PC Biddles, whom John Stallard instructed to accompany them.

At the house, having viewed the body of Ann Waring and examined Ann Barnes, it was apparent to Dr Stallard that both women had been poisoned, and he quickly began to look around for the source of the irritant. After asking a few questions, he directed Constable Biddles to take possession of the tea kettle and the teapots, then, accompanied by both of the young women, he returned to his surgery in order to make up some medicine which he sent back for Mary's mother.

In later years, police, under the direction of a senior officer, would have attended the house and much more would have been done to secure any available evidence. Unfortunately in this case, no more enquiries were made until the following morning. The girls were left at the house and nothing was done to prevent the possible disposal of any incriminating evidence. This apparent lack of efficiency has to be viewed in the context of the times.

The Borough Police Force, now under the command of Superintendent Robert Charters, had only been in existence for just over six years, and it was to be another five years before the creation of a Detective Department. In April 1842, the responsibilities of the Borough Police were still relatively basic – the preservation of the Queen's peace and the protection of the rate payers' property. Enquiry into crimes such as the one perpetrated in Oxford Street that night were very much the responsibility of the courts.

Around eight o'clock the following morning (Thursday), Martha Berry, a neighbour, told the coroner at the inquest into the death that the two girls were in the street outside their house talking to a group of women who had gathered to find out what had been going on during the night. She heard Charlotte telling the group that she had not been out of the house since eight o'clock the night before. Berry immediately challenged this, telling her that she was a liar, and that she had seen her and Mary outside the door at ten o'clock, arguing about going back into the house. She told the group that she had heard Charlotte say, 'You shall go in first', and Mary pushing her saying, 'I won't, *you* shall go in first, for there's sure to be something up.'

Barnacle, losing the sympathy of the group in the face of the older woman's antagonism, was forced to admit that this was in fact the truth, and then she made a show of pretending to be sick in the street, but brought nothing up. With the story of the tea now common knowledge, Martha Berry asked Charlotte if she herself had drunk any of the brew. In an attempt to regain some credibility, the two girls told the group of women that they had both taken some. Barnes had in fact studiously avoided drinking from the teapot and Barnacle, who claimed to have drunk a whole cupful, had only taken a sip from the second mashing.

The tension was not relieved when Constable Goddard arrived between nine and ten o'clock to arrest the girls. Typical of the times, one policeman had been sent, and in the absence of any form of transport, he walked the prisoners, accompanied by an ever-growing crowd, through the streets to the Station House in Town Hall Lane (later Guildhall Lane).

A somewhat bizarre situation now developed, as en route to the station, a running conversation took place between members of the crowd and the prisoners.

Sarah Boulter, a single woman who lived nearby in Grange Lane (also know at this time as Green's Lane), gave evidence both at the inquest and later at the trial, of talking to Mary Barnes who said to her that she and Charlotte Barnacle had had a word or two with Mrs Waring and that she (Barnes) had wanted to give the old woman some jalap. But Barnacle said that she would not give her any jalap, but a little arsenic to put her in

*After being arrested, the two women were taken to the Borough police station at the Town Hall in Town Hall Lane, which is now the Guildhall Museum.*

pain. Mary insisted that she had told her that '*that* would be *too* bad', but Barnacle said she would not give her enough to poison her.

Boulter told the Assize Court that Mary Barnes also said that Barnacle had asked her to go and enquire how much it would take to poison somebody and what sort of stuff arsenic was. Then Barnes went to Mrs Johnson's in Jones' Yard to ask the same question and went back and told Barnacle what Mrs Johnson had said. When they had got the arsenic, Charlotte told her that she would only give her half the compliment, and that *she took the paper of arsenic and scattered it into the kettle of water* but whether she put it all in or not, Barnes could not say.

At the time this conversation took place, the witness recollected that she and Mary Barnes were walking three or four yards from Barnacle, who would not have heard their discussion.

Apart from the minor discrepancy in her evidence whereby Ann Johnson told the court that both girls went to ask her about the arsenic, this conversation is quite interesting. Barnes appears to be doing two things at this stage in order to shift the onus of responsibility onto her accomplice. First, she insists that she only wanted to administer a physic to the victim, and second, that it was Charlotte who laced the tea kettle with arsenic, although in doing this she also makes a clear admission that she was present when the deed was done.

At the Station House, two of the chemists, Thomas Palmer and William Stephens, positively identified the young women as being the ones who had attempted to buy arsenic from them.

In the interval between their arrest and the trial, two things of minor interest occurred which are worthy of note. Following the hearing of the evidence at the inquest, the coroner made a scathing remark which gives a very clear picture of the low esteem in which the New Police, as the local constabulary were known, were held. (This was a national phenomenon as the British public had not taken kindly to having Sir Robert Peel, the Home Secretary's organised law enforcement agency imposed upon them.) The coroner commented:

> We have been told on credible authority that on the day they were apprehended, both made confessions to a Constable, admitting their guilt to the fullest extent. We always look with much disgust on such declarations of this kind, and there is generally a degree of sympathy for the parties when guilt is proved by conversations with a policeman or a turnkey. It savours too much of the French system for an English taste.

In view of the fact that at any future time right up to the end of their trial, neither young woman admitted to anything other than an intention to inflict some pain on their victim, the Coroner's comment appears to be valid.

The trial judge at the Assize made a similar, if less profound observation with regards to the questioning of the accused by the police. (It also underlines the perceived limitations of the police at this time.)

When William Goddard was giving evidence of arresting the girls, he told the court that he 'took both girls to the Station House and they both said they had not been to buy any poison. While there, several persons asked them if they had been to buy any poison. Barnacle was asked first – do not know who asked her.'

Mr Macaulay, defence counsel for Mary Barnes, immediately pounced upon this and declared that: 'It was a most unjustifiable thing for a posse of police to question the prisoner when she had no professional assistance.'

The judge, Mr Justice Patterson, then asked Constable Goddard whether he personally had questioned Mary Barnacle, to which Goddard replied that he had not.

His Lordship, apparently quite pleased with this answer, told the constable that he was glad to hear it. It was not the duty of a policeman to do so and he hoped he should not hear of it again.

The second point of interest serves to give a small insight into the prisoners themselves. In reporting the details of the inquest, at which both Mary

Barnes and Charlotte Barnacle were present, the *Leicester Journal* carries the following short rider:

> The conduct of the prisoners is very hardened and they seem to be altogether unconscious of the awful position in which they stand. The only observable alteration in their demeanour was that on their return to the Borough Gaol on Tuesday night after the [inquest] verdict they did not curse and swear as volubly as heretofore, but on that very day one of them had been in solitary confinement on account of having stolen a necklace and some articles of dress from a female prisoner. We are informed that the same girl on being seriously admonished by our worthy Mayor, hid her face in her hands to conceal her laughter.

The trial of Mary Barnes and Charlotte Barnacle took place at the Leicester Assizes before Mr Justice Patterson during the first week of August 1842. Having heard from all of the witnesses involved in the actual circumstances surrounding the purchase and subsequent administration of the poison, the final burden of proof as to the cause of death fell to John Pinfold Stallard, the surgeon who attended the house after Mary Waring died, and later treated Ann Barnes.

Dr Stallard's evidence was unequivocal. Mary Waring had been administered a massive quantity of arsenic which had resulted in her swift and violent death.

His son, Joshua Harrison Stallard, a surgeon at Birmingham Hospital, gave evidence of having examined the teapot, tea kettle and their contents. In the remaining half a pint of water in the kettle, he found five grains of arsenic. Four grains would be sufficient to kill a person, and the kettle when full would have contained between four and six pints, or at least eight times the amount he had examined.

Both of the Stallards – father and son – treated Ann Barnes during the three weeks when her condition was critical, and both were satisfied that she in turn had received a near-lethal dose of arsenic.

With the evidence laid before the jury, Mr Hildyard for the Crown sat down, having to all intents and purposes presented a *prima facie* case.

The two girls were each individually represented, Mary Barnes by Mr Macaulay, and Charlotte Barnacle by Mr Mellor. Both were competent advocates who now set to work, not necessarily to prove their clients' innocence – which would have been a Herculean task – but rather to extenuate.

Mr Mellor made play of the fact that a niece of the deceased, Ann Timson, who had been brought up by her, gave evidence that the dead woman's maiden name was Elizabeth Woodward, and she had always been known as Elizabeth. Mellor's opening shot was that the trial was invalid as the defendants were charged with murdering the wrong woman. This objection the judge swiftly dismissed. Next he asked that the jury ignore the validity of conversations, such as the one between Mary Barnes and Sarah Boulter en route to the police station, which he was legally correct in doing so. Finally, counsel put forward an emotive plea to the jury that it had never been the intention of the prisoners to murder anyone, and that this was a prank that went wrong. Both advocates inevitably challenged the forensic evidence presented by John Stallard (though neither was tempted to dispute the testimony of his son). Stallard had found massive corrosion and ulceration in the stomach of the victim, which was not typical of arsenic poisoning, and due to this, had not been able to specifically identify arsenic in what was left of the digestive system. However, his absolute conviction that the cause of death was due to arsenic was corroborated by two other surgeons, Messrs Bowmar and Young who had assisted at the post-mortem. (A further relevant factor is that the procedure did not take place until thirty hours after death which would have exacerbated the deterioration of the stomach and consequently created problems in performing the examination.) Macaulay even tried to introduce the possibility of Waring having died from cholera. Once more, the judge in his summing up imposed the voice of reason and directed the jury that the cause of death was not in any doubt.

For Mary Barnes, Mr Macaulay went along the route of winning over the sympathy of the jury. It was, he told them, 'one of those cases invested by a vast quantity of circumstances. It was an occurrence taking place in the lowest ranks of life, in this – in many instances – unhappy town of Leicester, and so far from divesting themselves of their feelings, it was to their feelings that he should address himself, and not to the cold method of legal calculation.'

In his summing up, the judge was explicit and unambiguous. It would be very difficult for the jury to suppose that the prisoners put the poison in the tea kettle believing it to be jalap or in ignorance of its real nature. The evidence clearly showed that they had enquired into the nature of the poison, that they bought the arsenic, and would have prevented the boy from labelling it if they could. They were also told that as much as would lie on a shilling would poison a person, and they had used such a quantity as would have poisoned many times that number of people. This was a case of murder; they only had to return a verdict of guilty or not guilty.

The jury retired, and after an hour, returned with the verdict that 'the prisoners were guilty of putting arsenic in the kettle but not with the intention of taking away life.' The judge told the foreman that this was no verdict and after a moment's consultation, a new verdict of manslaughter was returned against both.

On hearing the verdict, the prisoners broke down in tears, and Barnacle said that she hoped his Lordship would have mercy upon them.

Mr Justice Patterson, after a short summation to the effect that had the finding been one of guilty of murder, they would have both hanged, passed sentence on them 'that you both be transported beyond the sea to such place as Her Majesty may direct for the term of your natural lives.'

Macaulay's statement that this was an incident taking place in the lowest ranks of life is probably one of the most valid comments on this whole sordid affair. The two perpetrators were young and uneducated, both were illiterate, living in a squalid slum area where sickness was rife and life was relatively cheap. Little or nothing is known of their backgrounds, and the only insight into their characters is the incident in the gaol.

The two questions that need to be answered are: what was their true motive; and what were their intentions? So far as intentions are concerned, the trail which they left is very clear and easily discernable.

That they knew each other prior to Barnacle becoming a lodger at the house is almost certain. They came from a small area – George Carnall's comment, 'Why, that is Lot Barnacle' when he first saw her substantiates this, and if correct, begs the question of whether or not Barnacle's arrival in the household was part of a preconceived plan, although the dispute between her and the deceased certainly did take place.

If, as the defence proposed, it was only their intention to incommode Mary Waring, there were plenty of patent medicines and emetics on sale in the town that would have achieved the desired effect without in any way endangering her wellbeing. When the girls approached Ann Johnson, they did not ask how little arsenic it would take to upset a person's system; rather, they wanted to know how much it would take to kill someone.

It was at this stage that they told a deliberate and apparently unnecessary lie. They told Mrs Johnson that Mary's father had attempted to buy arsenic in order to destroy some bugs that were causing a problem to another lodger, 'Old Sukey'. (Susan Mee died of natural causes during the time between the murder of Mary Waring in April and the trial in August.) He had been refused and later went together with his wife and another daughter, Sarah, at which time they successfully made the purchase. Far from being irrelevant, this is the beginning of the prosecution's failure to identify a sequence of events which indicates the young women's true intent. Stephen Barnes and his wife always denied the truth of this statement, and the daughter Sarah had by the time of the murder left home and was no longer available to question.

There was also a perceived discrepancy in the timing of the defendants' visits to the town centre chemists. In the half hour between four o'clock and four thirty, first William Stephens refused to serve them and then they succeeded in making a purchase from Joseph Lockyer. They now had the means to commit murder – the question is, who did they intend to include among their victims? By Mary Barnes' own admission, she was present when Barnacle tipped the contents of the package into the kettle, sufficient, even after it had been replenished hours later, to kill not one but several people. No enquiry was ever made as to what became of the packaging that young Thomas Murdy prepared and labelled, but it is fairly certain that this would have been disposed of, probably by dropping it into the fire grate. Once again though, this is a glaring inadequacy in the investigation.

*Due to their illiteracy, neither Mary Barnes nor Charlotte Barnacle understood that any packet of arsenic that they purchased would be clearly labelled with the name of the dispensing chemist.*

Having done the deed, the two girls now needed to cover their tracks. At eight o'clock on Wednesday evening, Charlotte Barnacle and Mary Barnes attempted to buy another pennyworth of arsenic from Thomas Palmer in Market Street. Mr Hildyard, for the prosecution, chose to believe that this was a time slippage on the part of the witnesses, and that Palmer was mistaken. This was not just carelessness on his part; it displays gross incompetence and later allowed the prisoners to escape the correct verdict.

Thomas Palmer and his assistant John Burrell, both very credible witnesses, were adamant that the two girls were in the shop at eight o'clock. A third witness, Mr Collier, proprietor of the *Mercury* newspaper, could have corroborated this but he was never asked.

It is the logical conclusion that having laid the ground with the story to Ann Johnson about Mary's father previously purchasing arsenic, they now intended to make it look as if he was responsible for what was about to occur. Realising that it was possible someone might trace their purchase of arsenic during the afternoon from Lockyer's shop, they needed to replace this with another packet and be in a position to present it as their original purchase to anyone who might later enquire.

Here their illiteracy comes into play. Because they did not know what Thomas Murdy was writing when labeling the package, they would also not know that it was common practice to include on such a label the name and address of the chemist who supplied the item. Therefore, if they succeeded and at a later time were able to produce a sealed packet of arsenic, it would be obvious to anyone who could read that it was not the one sold to them by Lockyer.

The fact that they laced what was effectively a communal tea kettle immediately destroys the supposition that it was only Mrs Waring who was their target. This is accentuated by the fact that when the apprentice George Carnall was present with the girls in the yard, it was almost an hour before Mary Waring was due home, and continual reference was made to the fact that '. . . *they* are having it. . . *they* will taste it. . . be damned, *they'll* never taste it'.

Finally, while the old woman was dying and Ann Barnes, having drunk some of the tea, was violently ill, they deliberately administered two cups from the refilled kettle (which Barnacle had tasted and knew was still poisoned and which Mary Barnes refused to touch), to Mary's father, and Mary took another cup up to her mother, thus ensuring that both of them had also consumed two cups of the brew.

The murderous intent of the two girls is beyond dispute. The fact that this intent extended to members of the household other than Mary Waring, or that they were indifferent to the possibility, is also patently obvious. As to a motive, this will never be ascertained. A simple argument over a man visiting Charlotte Barnacle in her room is hardly grounds for murder. There is no indication that the old lady had any money or that any other advantage would result from her death. The house was rented and so nothing was to be gained by the deaths of Ann or Stephen Barnes other than if Mary's parents were removed and her sister Sarah were out of the equation, the story about Stephen purchasing arsenic would place suspicion squarely upon him.

Whatever the true motive behind the murder of Mary Waring and the near-fatal poisonings of Stephen and Ann Barnes, any chance of unearthing it disappeared forever when Mary Barnes and Charlotte Barnacle boarded the ship that was to transport them away from England and into obscurity for the rest of their lives.

# 3

# THE UNSOLVED DROWNING

## Constable William Henry Wells, 1906

The dead body of PC William Henry Wells, aged thirty one, living at 9 Dorset Street, was recovered from the Leicester Canal in the vicinity of MacDonald Road on Wednesday morning under mysterious circumstances. . .

Thus began the relatively short report in the *Leicester Advertiser* on Saturday 24 November 1906, which proceeded to outline the details of the inquest held at Leicester Town Hall by the borough coroner, Robert Harvey, into the drowning of Constable William Wells while on night duty earlier in the week.

A married man, the father of three children, William Wells joined the Leicester Borough Police Force as Constable 208 in April 1902 at the age of twenty-seven. Having worked, as was normal for new recruits, on the Central Division for a period of time at the Town Hall police station, in August 1906 he was transferred to the Belgrave Division which was on the side of town where he lived, and would make travelling back and forth to work easier.

Around nine o'clock on the evening of Tuesday 20 November, while he was getting ready to go to work, Wells' mother, Mary Ann Johnson, who lived a hundred yards away in Moorgate Street, arrived at the family home at 9 Dorset Street in order to be with his wife who was about to go into labour with their fourth child. When she arrived, her son was playing with one of the children and left shortly afterwards to take the short walk to the police station at the junction of Loughborough Road and Holden Street, where he paraded at 10 p.m. for duty along with the other night men before going out on his beat.

Unusually, there does not appear to have been any supervisory officer on duty at Holden Street. Throughout the entire night up to the time of his death the policeman was not visited by a duty sergeant or inspector. The district covered from Holden Street to the south – Belgrave – was a relatively small and compact area made up of a tight network of streets and terraced housing, and the men working the night beats could have expected to be seen by a sergeant at least once before and once after their meal. At the

Right: *Constable 208 William Henry Wells.*

Below: *The now derelict Belgrave police station at the junction of Loughborough Road and Holden Street.*

subsequent inquest evidence was given by a colleague, Constable Clarke, of seeing PC Wells when he reported for duty, and the fact that he was 'in good health and laughing and joking with the other men'. A possible explanation for this lack of supervision is that, for whatever reason, the Belgrave Night Sergeant was not on duty (he could have been sick), and responsibility for supervising Belgrave men fell upon the sergeant based at the next nearest station, Woodboy Street, and he did not find time to pull in the extra visits. PC Wells' beat extended from Law Street along Belgrave Road down to Abbey Park Road, and included the newly-built properties in the side streets backing onto the canal.

Around 2 a.m., a steady, persistent winter rain began which was to continue all night, and half an hour later PC Wells was pleased to see James Slater, one of the other constables, coming down Loughborough Road at 2.30 a.m. with a supply of hot coffee. It was the practice at this time for police officers to take their meal break, such as it was, out on their beat. (In later years, dependent upon how far they were from their base, men were allowed to walk back to the police station. Later still – after 1931 when the system of beat men working from Tardis style police boxes came into being – meal breaks were taken in the police box.) The refreshment system employed at Holden Street entailed one of the men returning to the station and preparing bottles of hot tea and coffee which he then walked around the beats distributing. On this occasion, Wells was fortunate; having walked up Belgrave Road to meet the coffee man at the corner of Cossington Street, he was the first to be served and his drink would have been good and hot.

Presumably while he drank his coffee in a convenient shop doorway or an entry, William Wells also ate a pack-up which he had brought with him (the remains of some bread and butter were later found in one of his top coat pockets), before continuing to work his beat, checking the houses and shops along Belgrave Road. (He also had responsibility for the Union Works, a machinery factory between Law Street and MacDonald Road.) In view of the size of this area, it would be reasonable to assume that the section along both sides of Belgrave Road, from the police station at Holden Street to Abbey Park Road on one side and the Great Northern Railway Station on the other, would be split into four or five beats. The last time William Wells was seen by any of his colleagues was at 4 a.m., when he and PC Clarke, who was working the next beat, met up by accident at the junction of Law Street and Belgrave Road. Both in good spirits despite the rain, Clarke commented that he had mistaken him for the sergeant, to which Wells replied, 'Same here.'

Two apparently unconnected events occurred during the early hours of the morning. Sometime between 3 a.m. and 6 a.m., Jane Butler, who was seventy-four years of age, living at 84 Marjorie Street, was awakened in the night by the sound of someone moaning nearby. She initially thought that it was her granddaughter who was in the next bedroom; and rising, she checked the

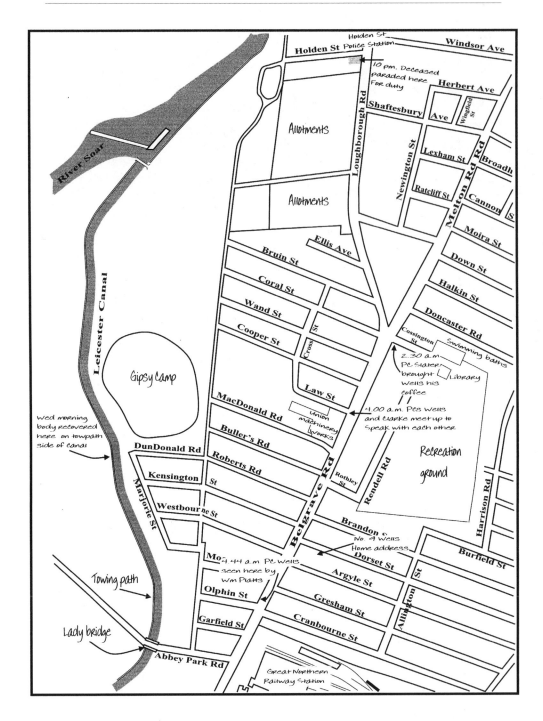

*The newly-built streets to the left of Belgrave Road comprised the beat worked by PC Wells on the night of his death.*

child and found her to be well and quietly sleeping. Mrs Butler then heard the sound again, but this time it was fainter and further away than the first. The woman was only able to judge the time as being between 3 a.m. and 6 a.m. because the street lights outside had been extinguished, it being the practice of the gas company to turn the lamps out between these hours in the winter.

Secondly, before a quarter to five, William Platts, a grocer's van man, who lived at 59 Law Street, was walking along Belgrave Road towards Olphin Street when he overtook the policeman who appeared to be studying something in his hand. As he passed by, Platts said to the constable, 'Good morning, there has been a lot of wet in the night.' Apparently startled, Wells replied, 'Yes there has. . . ' and carried on walking. This was the last time that Constable 208 William Henry Wells was seen alive.

When, at 6 a.m., Wells failed to report at Holden Street to sign off from duty, his colleagues became worried. The divisional superintendent, John Noton, who lived at the station, was awakened and a search for the missing officer began.

Once it was daylight, the canal bank, which ran from Abbey Park Road along the end of the streets which marked the boundary of Wells' beat parallel to Belgrave and Loughborough Roads passing the end of Holden Street, was checked. As there was no towing path on the Marjorie Street side, it was necessary to conduct the search from the opposite bank.

*Officers serving on Belgrave Division outside Holden Street police station, c. 1906. In the centre of the front row is Superintendent John Noton, the officer who found Wells' helmet floating in the canal. (Courtesy Leicester Constabulary)*

Soon after 10.a.m., Noton himself spotted Wells' helmet (identifiable by his number in the centre of the helmet plate) floating in the canal at the back of Marjorie Street near to Dundonald Road. The unpleasant process now began of dragging the canal to locate the body which was inevitably going to be lying on the bed of the canal. At this time, bodies were recovered by means of casting into the water a 'drag' which was a heavy steel-hooked appliance similar to a boat anchor tied to a length of rope, the expectation being that one of the hook's tines would catch onto clothing or the corpse itself, enabling the body to be dragged to the shore. Dependent upon where the drag hooked, the effects could be particularly deleterious, especially if the body was in an advanced state of decomposition. It was not until fifty years later, in 1957, that six members of the City Police swimming team were trained in the use of Siebe Gorman shallow diving equipment and an underwater search team was formed.

At 11.20 a.m., PC George Andrews threw the drag into an 8ft deep section of water near to the wasteland at the back of Dundonald Road. It locked onto a heavy object, and assisted by the other members of the search party, he hauled in the missing officer's body. Half an hour later a local doctor, Frederick Hutchinson, conducted an examination at the side of the canal and certified death. There were only two marks on the body, one on the side of the nose and the other on the right temple – both were post-mortem and probably caused by the process of recovering the body.

Although he was a fit and healthy man in his prime and a good swimmer, as he was dressed in a heavy uniform greatcoat and boots which were already sodden from having been out in the rain all night, William Wells would have stood little chance of recovering himself from the deep water. The puzzle was how he got to be in there, as the canal towing path where the body was found was not on his beat.

Numerous questions were posed both at the inquest and afterwards. None were satisfactorily answered, and now it is only possible to conjecture.

What was the noise that woke up Jane Butler? She heard moaning and initially thought that it originated from the next room, then decided it must have been out in the street; a few minutes later she heard it again, this time in the distance. The house at 84 Marjorie Street backed onto the canal, and the activity was very possibly not somewhere in the street, but at the rear, on the canal towpath. Did Constable Wells, on duty outside in a nearby road and in a better position to locate the source of the moaning, also hear the noises and, correctly identifying them to be coming from the canal, decide to investigate?

William Platts was very specific about what time he spoke to the constable. He said that the officer was studying something in his hand and that the time was 4.44 a.m. How did he know this? Could it be as simple as the fact that Wells was looking at his pocketwatch, shielding it in his cupped hand against the rain, and that although it was not given in evidence, Platts also enquired of him the time and was told it was 4.44 a.m.?

*Between the turn of the twentieth century and the First World War, in addition to the 'collar number' which police officers (and firemen) wore, the constable's number was also included in the laurel wreath of his helmet. (Courtesy N. Haines)*

The theory that it was his watch that Wells was studying is quite credible. Whatever the object was, it was small enough to fit into his hand. When the body was searched at the mortuary, in his pockets were found two notebooks, his gloves and stave, a pocket knife, pipe, tobacco tin, the remnants of his meal, and his pocketwatch which had stopped at 4.55 a.m. – eleven minutes after he spoke to the grocer's van man. Had the constable come into possession of something else, and if so, what and where was it? If it were important he would hardly have discarded it.

When William Platts spoke to him, Wells was obviously on his way directly to the canal towpath. In order to get to the canal, he had to leave his beat, go along Abbey Park Road, then down from the bridge onto the towing path. It was a dark winter's night, there was no street lighting and it would have been pitch black on the narrow path, but when the body was found, Wells' lamp was attached to his belt. He had chosen not to use it, making his way along the path in the dark.

If – another obvious possibility – he was simply going to a pre-arranged meeting with someone (and had been checking his watch to ensure that he wasn't late), then surely he would have used his lamp to light his way along the towpath, and also to signal his whereabouts to the other person.

Whatever was happening, William Wells wanted to arrive unseen, which means that the activity taking place was unlawful. At the inquest, a question was posed to Superintendent Noton by a juror concerning a gipsy encampment on the waste ground at the back of Kensington Street near to the end of Marjorie Street, which was part of the dead man's area.

*Juror:* Have you any caravans on the waste land now?

*Noton:* Yes, there are nine.

*Juror:* Did you see any signs of a struggle on the waste land?

*Noton:* No. I have questioned the owners of the vans and everything was alright during the night.

*Juror:* He had no business to be on the towing path?

*Noton:* None whatever.

*Juror:* Do you look after the vans the same as ordinary houses?

*Noton:* No. They don't pay rates and they usually look after their own property.

*Seen here is the winter uniform which PC Wells would have been wearing at the time of his death. The unwieldy greatcoat, wet with rain, would have made it virtually impossible for him to swim in the water of the canal.*

*Belgrave Road in the 1980s. The left-hand side comprised part of the beat that was being worked by William Wells on the night of his death. The white building on the right stands at the corner of Dorset Street, where Wells lived with his wife and family at no. 9. (Courtesy E.R. Welford)*

Whatever the events that led up to William Wells' death, they took place within a very short distance of that encampment. Jane Butler's house was in Marjorie Street, which finished in a dead end at the waste ground where the caravans were; and the sound of someone moaning possibly on the canal bank at the back of the house was a short distance from the site, and Wells' body was recovered on the towing path side of the canal near to the back of 84 Marjorie Street. From the outset, there was speculation that the officer had been killed by poachers whom he disturbed returning along the canal bank. If that is so, then one of them could have been injured, slowing them down sufficiently to give him time to make his way to the Abbey Park Road bridge. Here, the possibility that he was working on some previous information or knowledge that something was going to happen at about five o'clock can be discounted. If that were so, in view of the potential dangers involved, he would have mentioned it to Clarke on the next beat and arranged for the two of them to go together. In fact, this could be one reason that he was studying his watch. Officers working adjacent beats, which in this instance covered relatively small areas, would be aware of roughly where the next man should be at any given time, so he may have been trying to work out if PC Clarke was likely to be close at hand before deciding to go on alone. At this time, a constable who wanted to summon urgent assistance had two favoured methods. He could either blow his whistle (which in the event, Wells obviously did not have the opportunity to do), or in an area such as this, hammer with his truncheon on the cast-iron rain pipe that ran from gutter to pavement between each of the terraced houses. Either of these would be guaranteed, in the dead of night, to be heard by at least two other constables, and would have also alerted anyone down by the canal of his presence.

Did William Wells encounter a group of poachers returning from an illegal night's expedition, or gipsies from the encampment on the wasteland opposite up to no good? Was there a struggle and he was pushed into the water? Was he giving chase and fell in? Or did he simply, while creeping along the bank to find out what was going on, lose his footing and fall?

Whatever the true circumstances leading up his death were will never be known. His wife, with four children to support, was granted by the Watch Committee a sum which was the equivalent of one month's pay for each year of his service and would have amounted to approximately £290. Having heard the evidence, the jury declared that, 'there is no evidence to show how the deceased came to be in the water', and the coroner recorded an open verdict on the death.

# 4

# 'I SHALL SHOOT HER TONIGHT — AND SOMEBODY ELSE'

*James Stevens, 1911*

The murder of Frederick Greaves in the street outside of his home during the early summer of 1911 was one of those incidents which contained all of the elements so sought after by the media. The victim, a boxer, was a well-known local figure, and the killing came at the end of a violent domestic dispute that had stretched over half a day. The murderer, a close relative of the deceased, was already being pursued by the police who arrived on the scene just minutes too late to prevent the tragedy; and finally the question mark which has always hung over the incident was whether or not the dead man was the intended victim in the first place.

Because of the level of notoriety which the case attracted, certain conclusions were drawn at the time which, with hindsight, were not necessarily accurate, while some other details are, from an historical standpoint, worth examining.

The story begins in January 1909 with the marriage of Ann and James Stevens. Ann, at twenty, was two years younger than her husband, and initially, the couple moved into a terraced house at 33 Dorset Street, situated in the next road to Ann's sister and her husband, Fred and Alice Greaves, who lived in Argyle Street. The Greaves' were a little older than Ann and James – Fred being thirty, and they had five children, the youngest being just two years old. Fred Greaves was a good middle-weight boxer, and as such, a well-known local sporting figure. (In the years prior to the Second World War, boxers such as Reggie Meen, 'Pop' Newman and the heavyweight champion Larry Gains, trained in the upper floor gymnasium of the Jolly Angler pub in Wharf Street.) Out of the ring, Greaves was described as a quiet, amiable man.

James, slightly built and clean shaven, was an ex-soldier who, at the time, was still on the army reserve list, and as such received a pension each quarter of £2s 6d, which, to a young married couple, would have been a very welcome bonus. Meanwhile, the young man was employed as a shoe hand, a job which he lost a few months after the marriage took place.

He appears to have secured another job fairly quickly as a clicker in the boot and shoe trade, and twelve months after their wedding in January 1910, Ann Stevens found herself to be pregnant. However, about this time, she discovered that her husband of only a year was having an affair, and shortly afterwards found out that he was also involved with a second woman who was married. Not unreasonably, this led to a serious deterioration in their relationship and possibly prompted a move from Dorset Street to Newton Cottages in East Bond Street just off of Churchgate.

During the last week of April 1911, James Stevens again lost his job, and the couple decided to split up, selling the household contents and dividing the meagre proceeds between them. He elected to go to Kettering to stay with a cousin and look for work, while she, with their now eight-month-old boy, moved into lodgings with George King, a hawker, and his wife at 21 Bow Street, off Wharf Street, near to where she worked at Hill's boot and shoe factory.

Here it is worth pausing to look at one or two of the small details concerning James Stevens which are quite telling in relation to his character. Having been married for only twelve months, his wife pregnant with their first child, he was already having affairs with not one, but two women. Was the reason he lost his first job connected with this – that one or both of the women were connected with his work, or the wife of someone in a position to remove him? Why was he dismissed from the second job which he only held for a very short time? Ann Stevens, when interviewed in the middle of May 1911 by a journalist, specifically said, 'about a fortnight ago he was *discharged* from his employment. What had he done to warrant this?'

Leicester was at this time one of the biggest centres in the country for the boot and shoe trade. Men were coming from other locations in the Midlands into Leicester to obtain employment in the industry, so why did Stevens decide at such short notice to go to another town to seek work when there was ample employment where he lived? The obvious conclusion has to be that there was something in the circumstances of his dismissal to indicate that he was not going to get another job locally.

The couple separated during the last week in April, and something else here is very clear: Stevens did not leave Leicester to seek employment elsewhere with a view to summoning his wife when he had done so. They split up, the household effects were sold, and Ann took the child and moved on. Within a day or two of his arrival at his cousin's in Kettering, James sent a despondent postcard to her, care of his sister-in-law, Alice Greaves at Argyle Street, saying that he couldn't find employment in the town.

On Tuesday 9 May, James turned up unexpectedly at Ann Stevens' new lodgings at 21 Bow Street, again bemoaning to her that he could not find work. Although they appeared to be on friendly terms, he was not allowed to stay overnight with her at Bow Street and the next morning he left Leicester on his bicycle stating his intention of going to Norwich.

The following day (Thursday), Ann received a postcard at Bow Street from James saying that he had ridden 62 miles, was running out of money and had decided to return to Kettering. (He must have written and posted this card on Wednesday afternoon.)

Although Ann Stevens' new landlady, Ellen King, described the behaviour of the couple during this visit (she actually refers to 'visits' so he probably returned again to the house early on Wednesday morning, prior to Ann going to work and before his setting off for Norwich), as friendly, even affectionate, although this could have been a one-sided matter. Bearing in mind that, having caught her husband out in a couple of extra-marital affairs, and then splitting up with him within days after his dismissal from work, Ann might well have been attempting to deal with James' visits in a civilised manner. He, on the other hand, seems to have viewed things differently, as his card to her began, 'My Dear Wife' and ended 'from your loving husband'.

A picture begins to emerge of a man who has played the game and, having lost, is now reaping the consequences. He is unemployed and his wife has left him. Despite the move to Kettering, he is, within days, returning unannounced to see her, cycling all the way from Kettering to Leicester (a daunting task in itself, more than 25 miles on un-metalled roads, riding what, by modern terms, would be a very basic form of a cycle). He writes postcards to her, signed in endearing terms.

She, on the other hand, has a full-time job at a factory in Wharf Street, has moved into lodgings near to her place of employment, and has family support in the form of her sister Alice Greaves and her husband Fred, who lived within walking distance.

Something at this time, of which no one was aware, nor could reasonably have been, was that James Stevens was mentally unstable.

Having returned to Kettering from his unsuccessful quest for work, James Stevens decided once more on Saturday 13 May to mount his bicycle and make the journey to Leicester to see his wife. He arrived at Bow Street around five o'clock in the afternoon, and, on knocking at the door, was annoyed to find that although this was a half-day of work for her, and she would have finished about one o'clock, Ann had not returned home and their baby was in the care of a child minder, Mrs Stanyon.

Knowing the area and his wife's habits well, it did not take James Stevens long to track her down to the smoke room of a nearby local public house, the Three Cranes, at the corner of Humberstone Gate and Wharf street. He walked into the smoke room shortly after five o'clock, a few minutes after his brother-in-law Frederick Greaves, and found his wife drinking with her sister Alice Greaves, Alice's husband Fred, a friend Gertrude Makepeace (a single woman who worked as a weaver) and Ann's employer, Austin Hill.

## Rudge - Whitworth
## Britain's Best Bicycle

### The Right Way

to get the right bicycle is to get the new Rudge-Whitworth Cata- logue, the Cyclist's Encyclopeadia.

The new 76 page Illustrated Art Catalogue describes fully 106 new Rudge-Whitworths, explains the Constructional Details, has a Superb coloured frontespiece, and contains four unique charts of changeable parts.

It is sent Post Free from

RUDGE WHITWORTH, Ltd.,

### 72, HIGH ST.
### LEICESTER.

*By the turn of the twentieth century, cycling was one of the most popular pastimes for both the working class and gentry alike. It was still, however, quite a feat for James Stevens, on more that one occasion, to make the arduous ride along un-metalled roads from Kettering to Leicester.*

Angry at finding her there when, in his mind, she should have been at home with their child, James remonstrated with her and demanded that she immediately return home with him.

Here, for the first time, Ann Stevens comes into a bad light. She had decided after leaving work at lunch time, instead of going straight home, to go to the local pub with her employer and friends for a drink. By the time her estranged husband had found her, she had spent some considerable time in the pub and was somewhat inebriated.

Later at Stevens' trial, it was suggested by implication by the defence that in going out drinking after finishing work, Ann Stevens was a bad mother and that Stevens was merely attempting to get her to return home to look after their child.

This was not necessarily the case. Judged by modern terms, her actions in going out drinking rather than returning to her lodgings are questionable. However, these were not modern times, and the only recreational facility then for a working man or woman on a Saturday afternoon, after a hard five and a half day working week, was to relax in the local public house. At Stevens' trial, comment was made on the fact that the baby, not yet weaned, was still being breast fed. Defence counsel briefly made this point and then passed on, probably because he was aware that if challenged, he would find himself at a disadvantage. Throughout the week, Ann Stevens worked full-time at Austin Hill's factory in Wharf Street; consequently, on a working day, she would not have been at home to feed the child, who would have been in the care of a minder. On the Saturday in question, she had made arrangements for the baby to be looked after by a Mrs Stanyon. It was common practice at this time (especially among working-class women) for a working mother to leave an unweaned child with another woman who was still lactating and who would feed the child for her. Nothing is mentioned about Mrs Stanyon, other than that she was looking after the baby, but it is significant that when James Stevens made a final visit to 21 Bow Street late that Saturday night, he was told by Mrs King's husband that the baby was, 'well cared for and in bed'. Interestingly, in his attempts to get her to return home with him, James never once mentioned that the child might be hungry or in need of nourishment.

Events show that on that Saturday afternoon, Ann Stevens put herself in a highly questionable position which could be justifiably criticized; however, no direct evidence was offered to show that the child was neglected or in any way suffered due to her actions, which undoubtedly there would have been if such were the case.

Finding his wife drinking in the Three Cranes, and in the face of her refusal to leave and accompany him home, James Stevens' mental state appears to have deteriorated rapidly from this point. Within half an hour, he was back at Bow Street and was already in an agitated state. He told George King that he had found his wife in the 'Cranes', but she would not return with him and he declared his intention to 'get a gun and shoot the * * * * * *!'

Stevens spent the next hour and a half going in and out of the Three Cranes, badgering his wife to return to her lodgings with him. This she refused to do, either because she was enjoying the company or to make a point that having separated, she was no longer bound to do his bidding. Whichever it was, it is obvious that James became more and more angry as time went by. At one point, his brother-in-law Fred, in an attempt to defuse the situation, offered to get him a drink which he refused, preferring to buy his own beer. (According to Alice Greaves, while the two men were friendly, they were not always on the best of terms.)

This was in fact the only drink that James was seen to take, and having finished it, he went to where his wife was seated and told her loudly, 'You are sitting here laughing this afternoon, but you will not be laughing this time tomorrow. I am going away and I shall get the child's head and I shall bring it here and put it on the table,' whereupon he once more left the premises.

It was at this point that Ann Stevens decided that it was time to leave (it was now somewhere between seven and half past), and accompanied by her sister and Gertrude Makepeace, she made her way out into Wharf Street where James was waiting for them. Attaching himself to the group, he walked with them in the direction of Bow Street which was a few minutes away.

*The Three Cranes public house (now the Cork & Bottle) at the corner of Wharf Street and Humberstone Gate, where Anne Stevens spent the afternoon of the murder drinking with her sister and brother-in-law.*

Almost immediately they saw James' younger sister coming towards them, pushing their baby in what is variously described as a mailcart and a perambulator. This was obviously contrived, and James must have made the arrangement with his sister at some point during the afternoon.

Ann Greaves was annoyed by this charade, and taking the child from the girl, carried on walking along Wharf Street. The other two women, Alice and Gertrude, crossed over to the other side of the road to avoid the domestic scene that was rapidly escalating. They heard Stevens demand of his wife where she was now going, and when she told him that she was going with the baby to her sister's house, he became incensed and shouted at her, 'You are not!' He grabbed the pram and ran off with it into Bow Street.

A few minutes later, having deposited the child back at its mother's lodgings, James Stevens was again in Wharf Street, raging at the woman who was defying all of his efforts to force her to go with him. The two sisters and Gertrude Makepeace had regrouped during his short absence and when Stevens began to berate Ann, her elder sister intervened on her behalf. Losing control completely, James Stevens now drew a pocket knife and first stabbed his wife in the neck with it before slashing her sister's face. As passers-by tried to detain him, he shouted, 'I'll do the lot of you in!' and turning, ran away from the scene. An ambulance was summoned and the injured women were taken to the Leicester Infirmary. The time now was approaching eight o'clock.

A question arises here as to what James Stevens really wanted that afternoon. Not for the first time during their short separation, he had mounted his bicycle and undertaken the long and gruelling ride from Kettering to Leicester. Although throughout the affair, emphasis was placed on his apparent concern for the baby, he was actually aware that the child was being cared for. His obsession during the entire afternoon – and the cause of his eventual mental breakdown – lay in his attempts to get his wife away from the company she was with and back to her lodgings *with him*. At his trial, when summing up, the judge, Mr Justice Pickford, in reference to Steven's presence in Leicester that afternoon, made the comment, with a deal of perception on his part, that 'there is no doubt that the prisoner went there with the intention of getting his wife home. . . whether there was something more behind this, they [the court] did not know, and did not care to enquire.' Was it James Stevens' intention to get his wife on her own in order to make a last ditch attempt at a reconciliation, and his being thwarted caused him to lose all sense of reality?

Word spread very quickly concerning the incident. Wharf Street and the adjoining Belgrave suburb were two very tightly-knit communities and an occurrence of this nature was going to draw immediate attention. Within a short while, news of the knifings reached Woodboy Street police station where Detective Sergeant Edward Kendall, who was on duty at the time, gave instructions to the foot patrol men that Stevens was to be arrested and brought in. He himself set off to check the local pubs and places where the man might be biding his time.

Kendall was an experienced policeman and knew his area well (the following year he was to be one of the investigating officers in the murder of a prostitute, Annie Jennings in nearby Archdeacon Lane – *see* Chapter 5), and he rightly had two main areas of concern. First, there was a man roaming around his area with a knife who had already injured two women and constituted a serious risk to public safety. Second, this was a district where James Stevens' actions would not be allowed by the locals to pass unchallenged. Fred Greaves was a popular figure who might, under normal circumstances, be a quiet, amiable man, but he was also a renowned fighter whose wife had had her face slashed and his sister-in-law had been stabbed – it would not be long before he was out looking for the culprit himself.

Sergeant Kendall could not, however, have anticipated what happened next. While he was scouring the local pubs and dives, James Stevens was visiting an address in Mansfield Street near to where he had previously lived at Newton Cottages. He knocked at the door of a Mr Norman, who lived at no. 70, and introducing himself as a friend of Norman's son, told him that he was going shooting the following morning and asked to borrow a rifle which he understood that Norman owned.

According to Norman, Stevens (who was unknown to him), arrived at his house around nine o'clock, and at first he refused the request, but on being told by the man that he was a friend of his son's, eventually acquiesced. He gave Stevens a small bore rifle (probably .22 calibre) which was suitable for shooting rooks, along with sixty cartridges which were a mixture of long and short types, the short being for bird shooting, the longer carrying a heavier charge for rabbits. Now in possession of a firearm, Stevens once more disappeared into the gathering dusk.

Again this is something which must be questioned. According to Norman, he was in his home late in the evening when a total stranger knocked on the door and asked to borrow from him a firearm and ammunition on the flimsy pretext that he was 'going shooting'. With no enquiry or proof of identity, Norman handed him the gun – apparently no security was offered or asked for, and Norman, on the face of it, had no guarantee that he would ever see the weapon again.

Unfortunately, other than the fact that the premises were situated a few doors from a common lodging house, no record now appears to exist as to what sort of property was at 70 Mansfield Street, or who 'Mr Norman' was. The occupants of most of the surrounding premises are listed, and this absence indicates that Norman did not maintain a long-term occupancy. Mansfield Street, off of Churchgate, was on the edge of the Abbey Street/Belgrave Road district, renowned for its insalubrious rookeries and lodging houses. Whatever Norman's occupation was in reality, it is most likely that, having lived nearby, Stevens knew of him as a man who could, for the right price, be relied upon to supply a firearm.

In the meantime, Frederick Greaves was at the Leicester Royal Infirmary where his sister-in-law was receiving treatment for the stab wound in her neck – which turned out not to be serious, and his wife was having a number of stitches put into the knife wound in her face. They were joined there by Ann Stevens' employer, Austin Hill, and when the two women were discharged from the hospital shortly before ten o'clock, they got onto a tramcar in order to return to the Greaves' house in Argyle Street. (Hill lived further along Belgrave Road, in Doncaster Road, which was a few minutes walking distance from Argyle Street.) However, because of the women's distressed condition, the four left the tram in Horsefair Street and Hill put them all into a cab to complete the journey.

On their arrival at 180 Argyle Street, they found the house to be a hive of activity with relatives and friends of the Greaves awaiting their return. Among those at the house was Gertrude Makepeace (who lived only a few doors from the Greaves family, at 167 Argyle Street) and she put the time of the group's return to the house as being around ten o'clock.

Fred Greaves remained at the house long enough to drink a bottle of beer and gather his thoughts before, Austin Hill later told the Court, he suggested that they go out for a drink to get away from things. They walked off down to the nearby Horse and Jockey pub on Catherine Street. It is most likely that the true purpose for them leaving the house was in order to check around to see if James Stevens was in the vicinity. A short time later, they returned to 180 Argyle Street, and rejoined the group of assembled neighbours in the back parlour of the house.

Despite the lateness of the hour, James Stevens continued in his persistent visiting of 21 Bow Street. At ten minutes to eleven, he once more appeared there demanding to know from George and Ellen King if his wife had returned from the infirmary. On discovering that she was not there, he enquired what was happening to the baby, and was told that he was well cared for and was in bed asleep.

Either through bravado or agitation, Stevens now opened his coat to reveal to George King the rifle, and passing it from one hand to the other, next pulled some cartridges from his pocket saying, 'I shall shoot her tonight – and somebody else!' It is quite significant that he did not say, 'and anyone else who gets in my way.' He obviously had a direct intention that his wife and another specific person would be his victims. The hawker told Stevens not to be silly and persuaded him to leave his house, whereupon he himself hurried off down to Woodboy Street to tell the police that their fugitive was now armed.

Shortly after Stevens left the house in Bow Street for the last time, Joseph Wright Emerton, a young errand boy, was sitting on the front doorstep of 18 Argyle Street where he had been posted as a lookout, when he saw a figure approaching. At first he thought that it was another boy coming towards the house, and then when it was too late to raise the alarm, he realised that it was Stevens, crouching down in the shadows and moving along close to the walls of the houses with the gun in his hand. 'Where's Sis?' he demanded of the terrified youth. ('Sis' was the name by which Ann Stevens was often known.) Emerton replied, 'She's in the room.'

Stevens then questioned him in whispers as to who else was in the house, before tiptoeing past the boy through the open door into the front room. Covering Emerton with the rifle, he told him to 'Go in, but don't let them know I'm here.' The lad moved into a position between the two rooms where, seeing him, Gertrude Makepeace commented on how ill he looked.

His mother asked him if he had been on the roundabouts at the fair, to which he replied that he had. Desperate to extricate himself from the situation, Joseph now asked his mother for some money for chips and she passed to him a penny, whereupon he moved back into the front room. With the rifle still on him, Stevens now backed away to the door into the street. As he was about go through it, the boy heard a man in the room say, 'If he was here, I'd fight him.'

Stung by the comment, Stevens pushed past the lad towards the connecting door. Joseph made as if to return to his place on the doorstep, but while Stevens' attention was diverted, slipped out and crept away beneath the window to safety.

The boy's unnatural pallor had registered with Gertrude Makepeace, and ignoring the chatter going on in the room, she focused on his leaving and caught the sound of movement in the front room as James Stevens moved stealthily back in to see who had spoken of challenging him. She then realised that she was staring at the figure of Stevens in the darkened front room, the rifle up to his shoulder, pointing it into the assembly of people. Springing to her feet she shouted, 'There's somebody in the room with a gun!'

Stevens moved out of the shadows and said to her, 'You stand back', and he then moved out through the front door into the street. Austin Hill was nearest to the door, and going out, saw James Stevens in the road about ten or twelve yards away holding what he took to be a heavy stick. As he moved back into the front room, he was joined by Fred Greaves. Hill said to him, 'Fred, don't you go out, that fellow's outside and he's got a big stick or something of the sort, you'd better stay inside.' Greaves ignored him and went into the street and began to walk towards Stevens. Rolling up his sleeves, he said to Stevens, 'You are the man I want.'

Others, including his wife, followed him out of the house and saw James Stevens with the gun now held low, pointed at the man moving towards him. As the distance closed, firing from the hip, Stevens shot Frederick Greaves through the heart.

Once more attempting to evade capture, while those at the scene were recovering from the shock of what had happened, Stevens again took off but was grabbed by two men, William Arthur Healey and Charles Benfield, in nearby Gresham Street. Their attention was drawn initially to Stevens when they heard a cry from someone chasing him who shouted, 'He's shot a man!' Grabbing Stevens, Healey snatched the rifle away from him, and with Benfield, held on to him until they were joined by PCs Clarke and Shipman who were already in the vicinity.

Prior to the two constables arriving (Detective Sergeant Kendall was already in Argyle Street, having tracked Stevens to his brother-in-law's house, he arrived only seconds too late to intervene in the tragedy), Healey recollected Stevens saying to him, 'We parted a fortnight ago I shot the first ****** I saw.' On Benfield asking Stevens who he had shot, he replied, 'It's Greaves the boxer – I'm sorry for it because it's a worry for the old folks.' (The latter part of this apparently meaningless remark was never explained.)

On their arrival, it was PC Clarke who took Stevens into custody from William Healey, while Shipman took charge of the rifle, which he found had the hammer down (being a single shot weapon) and one expended round in the chamber. Detective Sergeant Kendall was next on the scene, and on searching the prisoner, recovered from his pockets the remaining fifty-nine cartridges. On his arrest, James Stevens told PC Clarke, 'I shot the wrong one, I intended shooting my wife, not the man who was shot.'

Here Stevens could be displaying a quickness of mind and the cunning that is so often evident in this sort of situation. Historically, it has been shown time and again that people who commit murder (particularly serial killers), while a part of their mind is totally controlled by the instinct to kill, on another level function very lucidly in respect to their own self preservation.

He initially said to Healey, 'I shot the first ****** I saw', which in fact was not true because Austin Hill stepped out into the street in his full view, and he allowed him to go back into the room before Greaves came out. To the policeman he said, 'I shot the wrong one, I intended shooting my wife, not the man who was shot.' Therefore for the future record, to the first police officer with whom he spoke, he made it clear that he had not shot Greaves with malice aforethought – a prerequisite for a murder charge to be sustained. Even at this stage, he knew that unless he put this notion into place, he was in danger of being convicted of murder, and would hang.

Later, when interviewed in custody by Detective Sergeant Kendall, he made a written voluntary statement in which he said, 'I am sorry he is dead. He was a decent chap. I intended to do my old woman in. If I had had a repeating rifle, I would have done them all in and saved one for myself. I hope Norman won't get into any trouble as I told him I was going shooting. Of course I was not going shooting, I intended to do my old woman in.' From an evidential standpoint, this statement is virtually worthless. First, a court would be directed at an early stage that they should not convict anyone on evidence derived from a voluntary statement made by a person in custody. Secondly, while full of platitudes about the dead man and meaningless talk of what he, Stevens, might have done, there is absolutely nothing in the statement within law to influence a jury. The statement which would influence a jury is the one that he made to PC Clarke at the scene – 'I shot the wrong one.'

James Stevens' trial opened on the morning of Wednesday 14 June 1911, at the Leicester Borough Assize, held in the Town Hall before Mr Justice Pickford. The prosecution team was Mr J. McMurdy MP, and Mr R. Rafferty. Mr V.M. Everard appeared for the defence.

Having heard the evidence of the relevant witnesses, Mr McMurdy presented to the jury the voluntary statement made at the police station by the accused to Detective Sergeant Kendall. In the statement, Stevens went into detail about trying to persuade his wife to return to her lodgings and to his going to Mansfield Street to borrow the gun. He then went on to say that he went to Argyle Street purely with the intention of asking her to come home with him, but instead of her coming out into the street, it was the deceased who 'ran out saying, "You are the one I want". I being terrified at the moment, leveled the gun and fired, with the sad effect of killing Greaves.'

It was, the prosecutor told the jury, for them to consider whether they could credit any such innocent intention on the prisoner's part. They should rather consider why he approached the house in Argyle Street in the stealthy manner that Joseph Emerton described, why he was making those careful enquiries of the terrified boy as to who were the persons in the back room, and why, if he only wanted once more to speak with his wife, did he stand in the front room with the gun at his shoulder pointed towards the people gathered together?

Next he drew attention to Stevens' admission that in the street, 'he leveled the gun and fired', and elsewhere, his declaration that, 'if I had had a repeating rifle, *I would have done the lot in* and left one for myself.'

Dr Walter Schuller of Clarendon House, Belgrave Road, gave evidence of attending the murder scene and certifying that Greaves was dead. He later performed an autopsy on the body and found that the fatal bullet had entered between the fifth and sixth ribs, passed through the pericardium, the left ventricle of the heart, the stomach, the liver and the left kidney, lodging in the muscles of the back. The bullet recovered from the body was one of the shorter cartridges, a fact which the defence proclaimed was an indication that the accused was conscious of using a projectile that would be limited in its capacity to cause harm. In fact, what the post-mortem evidence showed was that at the range at which Stevens had used the rifle, the effects were devastating, and that even firing from the hip, the range was point blank. (Mr Everard studiously avoided mentioning that as a trained soldier, James Stevens would be familiar with handling firearms and perfectly aware of the effects of a rifle fired at close proximity.)

For the defence, Mr Everard, as was to be expected, made much of James Stevens' apparent concern for the welfare of his small son. He was careful when referring to the separation not to mention the husband's peccadillos which were the basis of the domestic trouble. Rather, he phrased it that 'they [the couple] had agreed to live in separate lodgings, and were not separated in the sense that they never met or quarrelled, and it had been shown that they lived on affectionate terms. He mentioned that from the proceeds of the sale of their household goods, Stevens had bought his wife a suit as a present.

Taking a more objective view, along with the terms in which the postcard that he sent her were couched, the inference seems to be that it was James who was trying to force a reconciliation with his wife – there is nothing to show that she in any way reciprocated.

Again, as was expected, Everard laid strong emphasis on Ann Stevens' conduct during the day of the murder:

Unfortunately, on this afternoon, when the prisoner had cycled over to see his wife and child, Mrs Stevens seemed to have gone to the public house to spend the afternoon in the smoke room there . . . they had heard a rather sordid story of the way in which this afternoon began, for it appeared Mrs Stevens had been drinking for three and a half to four hours before the husband appeared.

During her evidence for the prosecution, when asked by the judge about her sister's condition, Alice Greaves had conceded that, 'She had had a drop.' The barrister continued, 'He did his best to get her home to the baby but she would not, and stopped some two hours longer, and was in such a condition that she had to take soda water to pull herself together.'

In respect of James Stevens' own conduct, his counsel now embarked upon an emotive discourse on how his client had been driven to distraction by the apparent waywardness of his wife: 'It has been given in evidence that the prisoner made certain stupid, rash remarks – but he asked the jury to judge them in the light of the statement he made about [Stevens] fetching the baby's head and putting it on the table. That these remarks were made in the frenzied state into which the prisoner had been driven by the events of the afternoon.'

Ann Stevens, by leaving work and going out drinking, certainly put herself in an invidious position, but the fact remains that she had made arrangements for the child to be cared for, and it is very likely that, rightly or wrongly, drunken or sober, that in that knowledge, she set out to wind up her husband who, unbidden, had arrived making demands that she went with him. At eleven o'clock that night, the child was safely asleep in bed at 21 Bow Street, where, other than the period when James Stevens had himself arranged for it to be wheeled down Wharf Street by his sister, it had been all day. The 'events' which Mr Everard referred to were engineered by the man in the dock. The frenzy of which he speaks was due to the accused's frustration at being thwarted by his wife's persistent refusal to bend to his will. Everard's asking the jury to disregard the prisoner's threats towards the baby because of his agitated state was decidedly flying in the face of fact. This was the man who, in the course of the next few hours, stabbed one woman in the neck, slashed another's face, and then shot a man to death.

Finally, in closure, the defence counsel set out to paint a picture of Stevens' actions in Argyle Street as those of a man who, with mistaken intentions, took a gun to frighten his wife and was then confronted by his brother-in-law, 'a powerful man, a boxer', and frightened, he pointed the gun, and in doing so, his finger tightened on the trigger and accidentally the gun was fired. (He patently ignored his client's other conduct at the house, or his expressed regret that he had not been in possession of a repeating rifle.)

If the jury were being influenced by the defence counsel's very persuasive submissions, the judge was not. He now intervened and took issue with Mr Everard. 'You are putting the case to the jury', he said, 'as if they must find a deliberate intention to murder [Frederick Greaves] before they can find him [Stevens] guilty . . . if you use a weapon like a rifle and kill anybody, you have got to show some justification or excuse to reduce that from murder.'

The defence, Mr Everard blithely contended, was attempting to show that at the time that he discharged the weapon, the prisoner had abandoned all intention of firing the gun at anyone at all – and certainly had no intention of hitting Greaves. For, of all the people in the house at the time, he supposed Greaves was the one with whom the prisoner was on the friendliest terms. He again put it to the jury that the gun was fired, not with the intention of hurting anyone, but with the idea of frightening Greaves, who was a powerful man and a boxer.

Mr Justice Pickford summed up heavily for a verdict of guilty of murder against the prisoner. He directed the jury that if a man took a deadly weapon like a gun and shot somebody with it, unless there was something in the circumstances to make it otherwise – that was murder. He dealt specifically with the accused's stated intention to shoot his wife, 'and somebody else'. While he did not personally think that Stevens was referring to Frederick Greaves, he could not accept the defence counsel's assertions that these were idle threats. If they were merely idle threats, why did he go and borrow a gun, load it, and watch the house where the woman was. It rather looked to him like a pretty fixed intention to do something.

In the final analysis, the facts were not in dispute and the verdict became very much a matter of who presented the most persuasive case to the jury. After a retirement of thirty-eight minutes, a verdict of not guilty of murder, but guilty of manslaughter was returned.

Not at all pleased with this result, Mr Justice Pickford told the prisoner that in sentencing him to seven years penal servitude, he had taken into account all of the surrounding circumstances, including the fact that he had slashed Alice Greaves and was seriously intending to kill his wife, and that he was not at all satisfied that this was a sufficient sentence.

It is fairly certain that in a later time, James Stevens would have been found guilty of murder while the balance of his mind was disturbed, and an appropriate sentence handed down. As it was, the jury had only two alternatives; manslaughter, which involved a prison sentence; or murder, for which the only penalty was death. Influenced by a very plausible and well-presented defence, they elected for the former.

That James Stevens intended to kill his wife and someone else that night is fairly certain; the question is – who?

For the defence to maintain that Fred Greaves was the one person in the house with whom the prisoner was on the friendliest terms was ludicrous – he had only hours before disfigured the man's wife with a knife.

Stevens' stated intention to kill someone other than his estranged wife can realistically only have been either Fred or Alice Greaves. There is no inference that anything improper was going on between Greaves and his sister-in-law, so this can be ruled out as motive. Ann Stevens and Alice Greaves were very close as sisters and it is possible that Alice, as Ann's confidante, had given her sister advice and support when the marital breakdown occurred, thus incurring James' intense dislike of her. On the other hand, by lending support to his sister-in-law, Fred Greaves, in the role of some sort of protector, could also have made himself a definite target. The one thing that is certain is that James Stevens did not hesitate to kill Greaves and was incredibly lucky to escape being hanged for his murder.

As a small postscript, at the end of the trial, Mr Justice Pickford awarded the sum of two guineas to William Healey, and £1 10s to Charles Benfield for the courage that they displayed in tackling James Stevens and disarming him, not knowing at the time whether or not he had reloaded the weapon in readiness to kill again.

# 5

# THE ARCHDEACON LANE MURDER

## Annie Jennings, 1912

During the 1800s and into the Edwardian era, the Belgrave Road district of Leicester was a byword for poverty and petty crime. It was here that in the 1840s – during the years of the potato famine in Ireland – immigrant workers and their families flooded to, filling the squalid tenements and populating the lodging houses around Abbey Street, known as rookeries. Over the middle years of the nineteenth century, the area was, on more than one occasion, the scene of rioting and street battles between the incomers and the established local population. Shortly after the middle of the century, the Corporation decided to bracket the district with two police stations, and in 1878, Sanvey Gate station came into being under the command of Inspector George Langdale, while the second, Woodboy Street station, under Inspector Hickinbottom, opened its doors two years later.

Nancy Jennings, a forty-nine-year-old prostitute who was always known as 'Annie', moved into the middle of this renowned trouble spot during the early autumn of 1911. A native of Birmingham, who was described by those who knew her as a stout cheerful woman, Annie Jennings took up her trade from a one-up one-down, two roomed house which formed part of the tenement building at no. 1 Court 'C', Archdeacon Lane. (Although she had only lived in Court 'C' a few months, Jennings had been in the general area about four years and was well-known to the local police.)

Annie was a woman of regular habits, one of which was that she was an early riser. Consequently, when around nine thirty on the morning of Wednesday 3 January 1912, she had not been seen up and about, neighbours began to wonder if she was alright. James McGregor, an ex-navy man who was employed as a caretaker for the four houses in Court 'C', became concerned, and sent his wife Janice next door to see if the occupant, Mrs Daniels, had seen anything of her. She did this, and from there went to two other neighbours, Lily Bannister and a Mrs Pallett. The three of them then went to Annie Jennings' house, and finding the door unlocked, went in, and having gone a short way up the stairs, they realised that laying at the top was a body.

Panicking, the women ran out into the courtyard and told James McGregor what they had seen. He then went to investigate and found the naked body of Annie Jennings lying near to the top of the stairs with her throat cut. Leaving the house, McGregor ran to the nearby Woodboy Street police station to report the matter.

The first police officer to arrive at the scene was Detective Sergeant Kendall who found the upstairs room in total disarray. Jennings, who was naked except for a pair of boots and stockings, was lying at one corner near to the door with her throat cut. The body was partly on a sheet and a blanket, both of which were saturated with blood. The sheet, which was beneath the woman's back, was tied under her armpits and pulled over her shoulders, indicating that the body had been moved from the bed and dragged to where it was found. Nearby on the floor was an enamelled washing bowl containing what appeared to be a large amount of blood. It was obvious that the woman had put up a considerable fight before her killer had finally subdued her. The walls were extensively splashed with blood, chairs had been knocked over, bedclothes were strewn across the floor and her body bore the marks of a savage beating. A bloodstained table knife was found by Kendall near to the window where it appeared to have been thrown.

The sergeant was soon joined by other officers, led by Superintendent Herbert Allen who, just over a year later, was to succeed John Hall-Dalwood as chief constable of the borough. Just after ten o'clock, Dr Kirkland Chapel arrived to examine the body, at which time he estimated that Jennings had been dead for some fifteen hours. Having certified death, the body was removed by a fire brigade ambulance to the mortuary at the Town Hall where later that day, Chapel and his partner, Dr Arthur Barlow conducted a post-mortem.

Death had been caused by a wound 4in long and 1in deep, extending from behind the left ear to the centre of the throat which severed the windpipe. In the violence of the struggle, it would have been difficult for the gash to have been inflicted from the front, and it was more likely that the killer had managed to secure her from behind in order to inflict the wound. At this point, there was disagreement between the two medical practitioners concerning the possible murder weapon. Dr Chapel was of the opinion that the injury could have been caused by the table knife found by Detective Sergeant Kendall; Barlow, on the other hand, was adamant that it could not. The time of death was now considerably widened to have taken place between eight and fifteen hours prior to the body being discovered, making the time of the murder sometime between 7 p.m. on Tuesday night and 2 a.m. on Wednesday morning.

Within an hour prior to death, the deceased had been subjected to a severe beating. There was heavy bruising to the right eye, upper lip and chin. Bruises to the abdomen and thigh were consistent with the victim being kicked. The most significant injury was a bite mark to the neck which was later to become the most bizarre feature of the case.

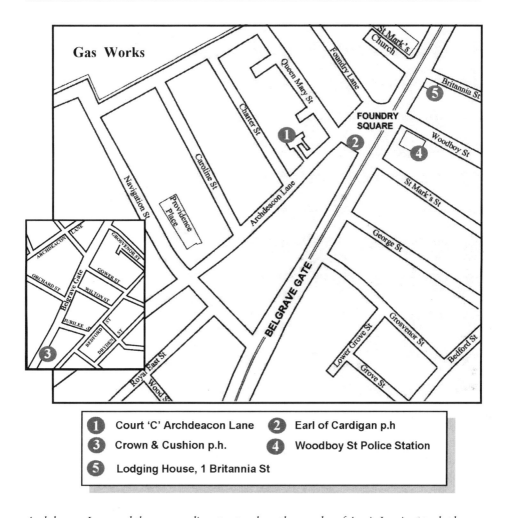

Gas Works

FOUNDRY SQUARE

1 Court 'C' Archdeacon Lane   2 Earl of Cardigan p.h

3 Crown & Cushion p.h.   4 Woodboy St Police Station

5 Lodging House, 1 Britannia St

*Archdeacon Lane and the surrounding streets where the murder of Annie Jennings took place.*

Herbert Allen put together an investigating team led by Detective Inspectors Smith and North. Their immediate task was to trace Annie Jennings' movements prior to her death, which, given her lifestyle and the nature of the district where she lived, was not difficult.

Enquiries established that soon after 11 a.m. on Tuesday morning, Annie called into the Crown and Cushion pub in Belgrave Gate where she got into conversation with a twenty-eight-year-old rubber hand named Archie Johnson, and a soldier who was with him. When spoken to by the police, the barmaid, Edith Halford, told them that Johnson had arrived in the bar first and was followed shortly afterwards by the soldier with whom he engaged in conversation; both were joined a short while later by the deceased.

The soldier, William Stanyard, a private in the York and Lancaster Regiment, who originated from Whitwick, was returning home on leave and had arrived in Leicester during the night at 2.10 a.m., en route to Coalville. For the next hour, the three remained in the bar talking and drinking. During this time, Johnson, who had himself served eight and a half years in the army and was still on the reserve list, produced an army document telling the others and the barmaid that he was going away the following morning to Yarmouth. Between eleven and twelve o'clock, Johnson later told Detective Inspector Smith that he left the pub to get some money, and on his return, made an arrangement with Jennings to later go back to her house.

There has been speculation that Archie Johnson and Annie Jennings were not casual acquaintances, but that Johnson may have been procuring clients for her. Although Edith Halford does not mention him leaving and later returning, if he did have an arrangement with the woman, it is very likely that he would have absented himself for a while in order to allow her time to talk Stanyard into going back to her room. Around 12.20 p.m., the soldier took his leave of the other two and went outside, and Annie swallowed down the remains of her drink and followed him. In order to give the couple time to make their way to Archdeacon Lane, Johnson spent about ten minutes in conversation with another customer who was an acquaintance, Edward Gamble – a night watchman who lived in the nearby Britannia Street lodging house at the corner of Belgrave Gate – to whom, before leaving, he gave his muffler to guard against the cold January weather. Archie arranged with Gamble that he would come back about two o'clock that afternoon; however, although the watchman waited until 2.30 p.m., he did not return.

Meanwhile Annie, who was well-known in the district, and Bill Stanyard, took a stroll along Belgrave Gate where they were noticed by Clara Lovett who, with her husband, ran the nearby Earl of Cardigan Arms in Foundry Square, and at 12.40 p.m. they were seen entering Court 'C' by Lily Bannister. Although Stanyard initially maintained that he was only with the woman for twenty minutes, this is not correct, as he was seen outside the house just under an hour later at 1.30 p.m., taking his leave of Annie. It is significant that almost immediately afterwards, James McGregor spotted her talking with a young man who was wearing a grey cap and brown boots. While McGregor did not know him by sight, this was undoubtedly Archie Johnson, who must have been hanging around waiting for the soldier to depart, before going back in with her himself.

Although they most likely had sex during the afternoon – just before three, Mrs Bannister noticed Annie fixing a pinafore across her bedroom window (which dispelled a possibility considered by the police that the murderer had done this), the events of the next hour or so provide an insight into their relationship.

Rather than a prostitute picking up and quickly servicing a client, they appear to have spent an almost domesticated afternoon together. About a quarter of an hour after Johnson arrived, Annie accepted a delivery of coal, following which,

*Number 1 Britannia Street. This bleak four-storey Victorian building, now a commercial premises, was until the mid-1960s a registered lodging house. It was here that night watchman Edward Gamble lodged.*

around two thirty, she went to the Earl of Cardigan and bought a shilling's worth of rum to take out, at the same time treating herself to a tuppenny shot of whisky. On the way back – it was now around a quarter to three – she called on Lily Bannister, asking if she would pay her rent to Mr McGregor. Bannister went over to the house to collect the rent money and Annie gave her 2s 6d. She saw Archie Johnson sitting on the couch and Annie told her that he was a friend who was staying the night. It was about five minutes after this that Bannister saw Annie fixing the pinafore over the upstairs window.

Annie Jennings was last seen alive that evening in the Earl of Cardigan at around eight o'clock, when she returned once more to the pub. There she bought some beer and whisky to take out, telling the barmaid that she had a client who was going to stay the night.

Following his lunchtime tryst with the woman, Private Stanyard made his way into town where, having joined up with some other afternoon drinkers, he was spotted around four o'clock going into the Barley Mow in Granby Street by Edward Gamble. The watchman joined the group in the pub for a short while before seeing the soldier off on the 4.30 p.m. train to Coalville.

Throughout the Victorian and Edwardian eras, the prospect of serving in the military as a common soldier was regarded as a lowly occupation suitable for the untrained and unemployable among the male population – it was only in periods of war and dire need that the foot soldier was elevated to the position of 'noble saviour of the nation'. Rudyard Kipling nicely encapsulated this sentiment in his poem, *Tommy*:

I went into a theatre as sober as could be,
They gave a drunk civilian room, but 'adn't none for me,
They sent me to the gallery or round the music-'alls,
But when it comes to fighting, Lord! they'll shove me in the stalls!
For it's Tommy this, and Tommy that, and Tommy, wait outside,
But it's 'Special Train for Atkins' when the troopers on the tide.

Consequently, after it became known that Annie Jennings had 'turned a trick' with a soldier, Stanyard became the prime suspect, and at the request of the Borough Police, by mid-morning on Wednesday, he had been arrested and was in custody at Coalville on suspicion of committing the murder. The soldier fully admitted that he was in the Crown and Cushion and that he had been in conversation with the dead woman and a man he met there who told him he was a reservist and showed him his mobilisation papers. He also agreed that he had gone with Annie Jennings to her room for sex. Desperate to distance himself from the affair, Stanyard told the police officers who travelled over from Leicester to interview him that he had only spent twenty minutes with her, which was untrue because witnesses put the time between his arrival in Court 'C' and departure as nearer forty minutes. Changing his story, he later estimated his time in her company as seventy minutes, which again was incorrect. Also he insisted that he had caught the 2.45 p.m. train, no doubt thinking that the earlier he said he had left Leicester, the less likely he would be implicated. With the time of death established as several hours after he was seen leaving the town, William Stanyard was quickly eliminated from the enquiry and released.

Attention now turned to the other prime suspect, Archie Johnson. Shortly after ten o'clock on Wednesday night, Inspector North, in company with Detective Inspector Smith and Detective Constable Roland Clowes, went to the house where Johnson lived with his parents, Eliza and Charles Johnson, and his sister Lucy at 28 Gray Street. Archie Johnson was upstairs when they arrived, but came down immediately when he was called. The conversation at the house

*The Barley Mow public house, a five minute walk from the LMS railway station and little changed over the years. It was here that William Stanyard and Edward Gamble spent the half hour before Gamble saw the soldier off on the 4.30 p.m. train to Coalville, thus eliminating him from the murder enquiry.*

was short and to the point. Inspector North asked the suspect, 'Where were you yesterday?' to which he replied, 'I was down at that woman's who killed herself', whereupon he was arrested and taken to the police station.

Archie Johnson was on the army reserve list, and as such, liable to be recalled, which was how he said that he got into conversation with William Stanyard. He was presently employed at St Mary's Mills as a rubber hand, and on the day of the murder, got up at 5 a.m. and went off to work with his brother. On the way, they called in at a public house for a drink (this was not unusual as it was not until the early part of the First World War that controls on the sale of alcohol were imposed), and the pair remained so long that they were locked out of work. The day before, Monday, he had received £2 6s reserve pay, of which he repaid 13s 6d on a debt that he owed and gave his mother £1 3s, and was left with 10s. Having first returned home, later in the morning he went into the town and, after visiting several pubs, went with Stanyard to the Crown and Cushion where they met Jennings. Here is the first anomaly: Edith Halford was definite that Johnson arrived in the bar alone and was then followed in by Stanyard. Had Archie Johnson, in fact, been touring the local pubs with the soldier looking for Jennings, and on arrival at the Crown and Cushion, told him to hang on while he nipped in to see if she was there, and then decided to have a drink and wait for her? He next told the police that having met her in the pub at around eleven o'clock, he went off to get some money and returned at twelve o'clock when Jennings invited him home with her. After 'being down for an hour' at the house, she told him 'to be off' and he left around 4.15 p.m., arriving home at Gray Street (which, being in the Oxford Street district of the town, would take a while to walk to) at 5p.m. It has to be supposed here that Johnson's reference to 'being down for an hour' is a figure of speech, as even he must have realised that the timescale involved far exceeded an hour.

The interview evidence here is patchy, to say the least, and leaves a lot to be desired. No mention is made of the fact that Annie Jennings left with the soldier, or that rather than leaving the pub with her himself, Johnson remained talking to Edward Gamble for some minutes, then waited in Court 'C' until Jennings had seen the soldier off of the premises.

When interviewing him at the police station, Inspector Smith asked Johnson what time he had left Jennings' house. Johnson replied, 'A quarter past four, and I arrived home at five and did not go out again that night.' This statement conflicts directly with the evidence of Alfred Hurst, a shoe hand who also worked at the Crown and Cushion. He said that he was present at lunchtime when Johnson and Stanyard were drinking with Jennings. He further told the police that at 8 p.m. the same evening, Archie Johnson came into the vaults of the Crown and Cushion and drank a pint of beer before leaving. Hurst said that Johnson was wearing a light coloured shirt which was dirty, and his muffler was missing. Although Johnson spoke briefly to another customer, he was in a hurry and appeared to be agitated. Despite the fact that this piece of evidence was crucial to the case (Hurst apparently did not personally know Johnson as he subsequently identified him at the coroner's inquest, having previously failed to recognise him in a police identity parade because he had said the man there was dressed in a woollen dicky which altered his appearance), nowhere in the interview with him or later at his trial was Johnson questioned about this disparity.

Another omission seems to be that no enquiries were made to check Archie Johnson's story when he showed Stanyard the paper allegedly ordering him to report to the military in Yarmouth on Wednesday. (Although Stanyard, as a soldier himself, would be expected to recognise the document, there is no guarantee at this particular time that, with limited schooling, he could read very well, if at all.) Johnson told the police that on the day of his arrest (when according to his earlier story he should have been en route to Yarmouth), he had felt ill and stayed in bed, and got up during the afternoon then returned to bed again later, which is where he was when the three detectives arrived to arrest him. Was the story of the recall true, or was he already planning to kill Annie Jennings and preparing a story to cover his possible disappearance after the murder? He certainly ensured that the barmaid Edith Halford overheard him saying that he was going away.

It is obvious that Herbert Allen, who was ultimately in charge of the enquiry, was satisfied that he had sufficient evidence against Johnson to make a case at court. The shoe hand was charged with the murder of Annie Jennings and remanded in custody for trial at the next Assize.

*Seen here shortly after he became Chief Constable of the borough in 1913, Herbert Allen was the detective superintendent in charge of the investigation into the death of Annie Jennings.*

The only conceivable reason for the failure of the detectives to pursue the apparent lie told by the accused as to his whereabouts on the night of the murder – an inexcusable error both on the part of the police and the prosecuting barrister – was that Superintendent Allen thought that there was other evidence which was conclusive – forensic evidence.

Unfortunately, the bloodstained table knife that had been recovered by Detective Sergeant Kendall was of little use to them. From the outset, there was a conflict of opinion between the two doctors involved as to whether or not this could be the murder weapon. The science of fingerprint identification was still in its infancy and not at the time being employed in Leicester. Similarly, police photography was still at a basic stage and Sergeant Hart told the coroner's court that due to poor lighting in the room in Archdeacon Lane, he had been unable to take a photograph and instead had made a hand-drawn sketch.

What the investigation now focused upon was the bite mark inflicted on Annie Jenning's neck, which was slightly under 1½in in length from the top of the upper jaw impression to the bottom of the lower jaw, and which, it had been agreed by doctors Chapel and Barlow, was human.

On Thursday 4 January, the day after being charged with the murder, while still in police custody, Archie Johnson was handed a pad of blotting paper by Detective Inspector Smith and instructed to bite into it. The resulting bite mark was to become the prosecution's central piece of evidence. The next day, Friday 5 January, Dr Chapel removed from the body of Annie Jennings the area of flesh surrounding the neck wound and prepared it as an exhibit at the forthcoming trial.

Additionally, there was felt to be substantial evidence contained in the bloodstains that were found on Johnson's clothing. At the time of his arrest, Inspector Smith noted that Johnson was wearing a clean shirt that appeared to have been recently washed. While at the police station, the suspect's clothing was taken from him and Smith noted that, 'his limbs from the ankles up were extremely clean while his feet were dirty, which gave the appearance that the body had been washed from the feet upwards'. His clothing, including a dark grey coat and a pair of trousers, was sent to St Mary's Hospital in London for examination by Dr William Henry Wilcox, the senior scientific analyst for the Home Office.

Dr Wilcox's findings were significant. On the front of the coat between the left pocket and the bottom button hole were several small stains of human blood. In other areas of the coat, he found a further nine stains. Inside the legs of the trousers were several smears of blood that were consistent with the cloth having come into contact with a bloodstained object. In his opinion, the staining could have been caused if the legs of the wearer had had recent blood on them. Here again, while Dr Wilcox could say that the bloodstains were recent, the science of the day was not sufficient to take the investigation one step further. It had only been eleven years since the Austrian Karl Landsteiner had discovered the fact that different human blood groups existed, and the integration of this knowledge into forensic science was still a thing of the future; consequently, it was not possible to directly link the staining to Annie Jennings.

Archie Johnson's trial took place during the first week of February before Mr H.F. Dickens KC, Commissioner of Assizes; the prosecution was undertaken by Sir Ryland Atkins, and Johnson was defended by G.W. Powers. A not guilty plea was entered, and due to the nature of the evidence, the court was cleared of ladies.

Dr Chapel gave evidence that on 5 January, he removed from the deceased's body an area of skin and fat at the place where the teeth marks occurred. He had compared these teeth marks with those on blotting paper taken the day before from the accused, and in both cases the curve of the upper teeth was similar. The last tooth on the right side of the upper jaw had penetrated the woman's flesh and the corresponding tooth on the blotting paper was triangular in shape, coming to a point which would probably have penetrated the skin in a similar manner. In the impressions on the skin there was a gap caused by the absence of a tooth – a similar gap was present on the blotting paper. Chapel said that he had examined the prisoner's mouth and found that the accused had a tooth missing in the same place as on the wound and the blotting paper.

Evidence was then given by Edward Rose, a local dentist who confirmed that he had examined both the flesh and the blotting paper and in his opinion, the likelihood of them being made by different people was remote. Why Rose, a well respected local dentist (who, a short while later in August 1914, was part of a group of Leicester practitioners who offered, free of charge, to examine the teeth of local men to ensure that they would pass as fit for the army), was not initially engaged to take the impression and prepare the evidence, rather than a police officer and the doctor, is a matter of speculation.

It was from a different direction that G.W. Powers, for the defence, launched a challenge against this piece of evidence. First he questioned the fact that the prosecution had elected to use a photograph of the wound in court when it was possible, as the flesh had been excised, to use the original material. Here Dr Chapel pointed out that while the flesh was preserved in formalin, due to deterioration (it had not been removed for preservation until a week after death occurred), the shape had now altered. Powers exploited this to its full, making the point to the jury that after this length of time, it was not possible to conclusively match the physical evidence to that on the blotting paper.

In respect of the bloodstained clothing, Johnson explained that he only had one suit, which on the night of his arrest he had put on. He was, he said, a regular football player and in playing, he often sustained kicks to his legs which bled – this, he averred, would be how the human bloodstains came to be on his trousers – they were his own. Again, despite the fact that the Home Office analyst described the blood as being quite fresh, and Inspector Smith gave evidence that when he examined the accused there were no recent cuts or abrasions on the man's body, the defence had done enough to throw in an element of doubt. (As with the teeth, it would have been better from the outset to have had the accused examined by a medical practitioner whose evidence would have carried more weight than the observations of a police officer.)

After a thirty-five minute retirement, the jury returned a verdict of not guilty, and Archie Johnson was once more a free man.

There can be little doubt that Archie Johnson murdered Annie Jennings in her room on the night of Tuesday 2 January. The real mystery is why?

Whether or not he was bringing clients to her and sharing her earnings will never be known. That they knew each other previously is fairly certain. Archie engineered the meeting between Annie Jennings and the soldier, he knew to wait in the courtyard near her house until the woman saw Stanyard off, and indicated that the coast was clear for him to go in. He remained for the afternoon – as Lily Bannister stated, being introduced by the deceased as a friend who was going to stay the night. Although Johnson returned to his parents' house around teatime, if Jennings is to be believed, when she told the barmaid at the Earl of Cardigan that she had a client staying the night, then they had arranged for him to return. This is borne out by Johnson going into the Crown & Cushion and having a quick pint of beer about the same time that Jennings was in the Earl of Cardigan. Alfred Hurst had described Johnson as being agitated. It was too early for him to have killed the woman and to be taking a drink to calm his nerves, so it is more likely that he was on his way to see her, and what was mistaken for agitation was, in fact, excitement.

What actually happened in the bedroom at No.1 Court 'C' in Archdeacon Lane can only be a matter for conjecture. Earlier in the day, the atmosphere between the couple appeared to be quite harmonious. There was no indication that Jennings' clothing had been removed forcibly, or that she was raped; therefore, it is reasonable to assume that she was voluntarily naked (apart from her boots and stockings, which she either intended to keep on, or was about to take off when attacked) at the time of her death. Robbery was not a motive, as when the body was removed to the mortuary, there were found to be two half crown pieces in her stocking.

No one heard the sound of raised voices coming from the room, which would have indicated an argument of some sort, although the next day, one of the women living in the Court, a Mrs Rigley, told the police that sometime in the night she had heard screams but ignored them. This latter comment could actually account for the neighbours' concern about Annie Jennings early the next morning. If Rigley had heard screams and ignored them, it is highly likely that the others did likewise. In going to see if Annie was alright, there may well have been an element of conscience as well as concern. This omission was, however, symptomatic of the area. When later asked for his view, Detective Sergeant Kendall told the court, 'in this neighbourhood even if there had been shouting no notice would have been taken of it . . . if we took notice of every cry of murder, we should be going into houses every night.'

*Over the years, the city end of the Belgrave district has been completely altered by the flyover and link road completed in 1975. To the right of the flyover in the background can be seen the spire of St Mark's church, a few yards from the house where Annie Jennings lived in Archdeacon Lane.*

Whoever killed Annie Jennings would have been, without question, heavily bloodstained, as would any clothing that they were wearing. Archie Jennings' clothing carried a small amount of blood spots on the coat – probably from spattering around the room. His trousers were stained on the *inside*, indicating that they had been pulled up over bloodstained legs. According to Detective Inspector Smith, when he examined Johnson at the police station 'his limbs from the ankles up were extremely clean while his feet were dirty, which gave the appearance that the body had been washed from the feet upwards.' In the room was an enamelled bowl containing blood. Here again there is another gap in the evidence. This was a two-roomed house (one-up, one-down), with no bathroom. It was the practice at this time in such households to keep handy a bowl of water for washing. Did this bowl in fact contain heavily bloodstained water? Jennings was naked when she was killed – the evidence from Johnson's clothes makes it reasonable to presume that he also was naked – and that after slashing the woman's throat, he sluiced himself down with water from the bowl and then put back on his clothes. It is most likely that next, he dragged the body onto the sheet on which it was found, and pulled it towards the door leading onto the stairs with the intention of taking it away and concealing it, but realising that this was impracticable, simply left it where it was and departed. Again, Detective Sergeant Kendall gave evidence that there was no light in the yard – it was a winter's night and it would have been easy for anyone to slip away undetected.

In respect of the bite on the dead woman's neck and the beating that she received before being killed, these are things that will never be resolved. Were they done in a sexual frenzy, or having begun to engage in sex, did something go wrong which threw the killer into an uncontrollable rage?

On the cold, rainy afternoon of Monday 8 January, a large crowd of people gathered at the rear of the Town Hall to await the removal from the police mortuary of Annie Jennings' coffin, to be taken on its last journey to her final resting place at Gilroes Cemetery. The necessity of a pauper's funeral had been avoided by a collection gathered from her friends and neighbours to pay the undertakers. The crowd was respectful and orderly, giving the twenty constables present little to do. As the cortege moved off, it was followed by those present as far as Belgrave Gate, where the mourners dwindled rapidly in the face of a sudden downfall of sleet and snow.

Whatever the answer to Annie Jennings' death, following Archie Johnson's acquittal, no further enquiries were made to find any other culprit.

# 6

# A GAMBLER'S END

Arnold and Edith May Warren were married in 1906 and lived quite happily together (although Warren later asserted that they had never 'hit it off') on the Hinckley Road side of town for the next seven years. Despite the birth in 1912 of their son James, at the end of 1913 things began to deteriorate between the couple, due to Arnold's newly found addiction to horse racing.

As in so many cases, Warren, who was employed by Wilkinson's of Little Holme Street as an engineering turner, soon found himself in debt, with a County Court order against him, a situation which led to arguments and disputes between him and his wife. Matters came to a head at the beginning of May 1914, when, during a heated row, Warren knocked his wife to the ground and kicked her. The following day, Saturday 2 May, he threw a loaf of bread at Edith, before attempting to strangle her.

Packing her bags and taking the baby, Edith Warren left her husband and took lodgings with her aunt at Cromwell Cottages in Dannet Street. Deciding to end the marriage and protect herself from further violence, she then committed what, in Arnold Warren's view, was an unforgivable sin. She took him to court.

Appearing at the Town Hall before the borough magistrates on 27 May to answer a summons taken out by his wife for assault, Arnold gave his address as 104 Dannett Street. After Edith Warren's complaint had been heard, Warren was asked by the chairman of the bench if he could not give up his addiction to gambling, to which he replied, 'I cannot, I have not got the willpower.'

Mrs Warren went on to tell the court that the basis of the dispute, culminating in the assault, was that her husband was seriously in debt and had sold up their household furniture and goods in an attempt to pay back some of the money he owed.

On examining Warren's financial situation, the court found that he earned 37s a week, and owed £18, or the equivalent of ten weeks' wages. Edith Warren made an offer to the court that she was prepared to live apart from her husband and take custody of their child if the court would make her a reasonable allowance to do so. This the magistrates agreed to, and ordered Warren to pay her 10s a week for the upkeep of his wife and child. At later hearings, this arrangement led to some minor confusion insomuch that at Warren's committal and his subsequent trial, the courts were told that Mrs Warren had been granted a Separation Order, which was not the case.

Although described by those who knew him as being 'of a quiet disposition, and a keen sportsman who played both cricket and football', Arnold Warren, plagued by the problems of his gambling and resultant debts, also displayed a violent and vindictive side to his nature. Having previously assaulted his wife, he now became deeply resentful of the indignity inflicted upon him by her having brought him before the magistrates to account for his actions. It was this resentment that was very soon to cost their son James his life.

In the weeks between his court appearance and the middle of July, Warren moved into lodgings at 98 Leamington Street, and continued to put such money as he had into horse racing. His lifestyle interfered with his work, and he now lost his job, which served to fuel his resentment towards the world.

Friday 10 July was Arnold Warren's thirty-second birthday. Jobless, in debt and alone, he decided to make one last effort to resolve matters. Going to the bookmakers, he placed one final bet on a horse called Early Hope, running that afternoon at Haydock Park. If it won, he would cover his debts; if it lost, then he was destitute. In case it should be the latter, on leaving the bookmakers, he went to a nearby chemist shop and purchased a bottle of laudanum with which to commit suicide.

The horse lost, and by early evening Warren had decided his fate. Recently, he had taken to visiting the Fosse recreation ground where his son was taken each evening by a child minder for some air before bedtime, and it was there that he made his way to.

Because she was out at work full-time, Edith Warren had, since separating from her husband, come to an arrangement with Arnold's mother, Mary Elizabeth Warren, with whom she remained on good terms, to leave the baby with her at 48 Gaul Street during the day. The arrangement was that at the end of the afternoon, the child was picked up by a local girl who took him to the recreation ground for a while, and then returned him home.

At half past five that afternoon, James was collected from his grandmother's house, as usual, by eleven-year-old Elizabeth Kate Skidmore, who lived in nearby Vorley Street. The girl took the child in a mailcart (perambulator) to the recreation ground where she saw Warren sitting on the grass. This was not an unusual occurrence; since their separation he had, on more than one occasion, been at the park in order to take the opportunity to play with his son.

Warren asked Elizabeth Skidmore if she would take a note back to his mother's house for him, asking if he could borrow a saw, while he looked after the child. Because she knew Warren was used to seeing the child in the park, Elizabeth readily agreed, and left James playing with his father. On her return from Gaul Street some time later, the mailcart was where she had left it, but Arnold and James Warren were missing.

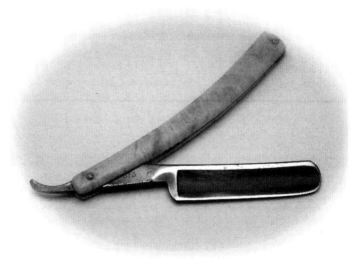

The next sighting of the two was at eight o'clock that evening by a courting couple, Stanley Frederick Hackney, who lived at 76 Law Street in the Belgrave district, and Alice Bray, a local girl from 34 Andrews Street. The couple were returning across the fields from Western Park (this area still being very rural, the 78 acre park, opened by HRH The Prince of Wales only seventeen years before, in 1897, was still surrounded by open ground), when near to the Home for Incurables, they saw what Alice Bray described as, 'a man and something white laying side by side'. On closer examination, they saw that the man was holding a bottle in his hand and that the child was dead.

Not sure whether the man was alive or dead, they hurried off to get help, and encountered a man named Albert McArthur, and sent him to find a policeman. Within a short time, Constable Harry Ashburner, who was on duty in Fosse Road, arrived on the scene. On his arrival, Ashburner found, as he later described, lying on his side near to the hedge in the second field on the left past the convent, Arnold Warren, a bloodstained open razor under his left arm and the blue laudanum bottle still in his hand. He was alive but unconscious; beside him James Warren, his throat cut, was obviously dead.

Harry Ashburner, who had been a policeman for only two years at this time, was a most capable young man, and having sent for a doctor, next administered a quantity of milk to Warren, which caused him to vomit up most of the laudanum, thus saving his life. When he came round, his words to the policeman were, 'Oh why didn't you let me die?'

By the time Ashburner had resuscitated Arnold and summoned the fire brigade ambulance, Dr C.W. Moore, a local physician, had arrived and certified that James Warren was dead. The officer now arrested Arnold Warren and, having arranged for the body of the child to be removed to the police mortuary, took his prisoner to the Borough central police station at the Town Hall. Here it was realised that with the boundary between the borough and the county being the first field in from Glenfield Road, the crime came under the jurisdiction of the County Police. Arnold Warren was moved later that night to the County Police headquarters at 4 Market Street and handed over to them for charging.

Warren's appearance before the Castle Court for committal to the Assizes was on Friday 24 July. Mr Donald Prynne appeared for the director of public prosecutions; Warren was not represented.

During the prosecution's opening address, when Mr Prynne, referring to the manner in which the prisoner had got rid of the girl from the recreation ground by sending her away with a note, told the court that Warren had said to her that, 'she need not make haste. . . ' The prisoner, who was at this point defending himself, suddenly interrupted, and called out loudly, 'That is a lie!' Told by the clerk of the court to be quiet, he said abruptly, 'Well he shouldn't tell lies!'

Having outlined the details of the prosecution case, Mr Prynne called as his first witness Elizabeth Skidmore, who told the court how she had taken the little boy to the recreation ground and, in order to run the errand for Warren, had left the child in his care.

Warren, in cross-examination, asked her: 'On the two or three nights previous to the Friday, as I took the baby away, didn't I promise you anything?' She replied, 'Yes.'

The chairman, concerned by the prisoner conducting his own defence, intervened and asked Warren, 'You have no one appearing for you?' Warren replied, 'No Sir, I have had no communication with anyone at all over it yet.'

Warren then continued, addressing himself to the witness:

*Warren*: When you came on the park didn't I call you straight to me as I sat on the grass?
*Skidmore*: Yes.
*Warren*: And I gave you two dozen or thirty photos out of cigarette packets.
*Skidmore*: Yes.
*Warren*: You stated before that when you first came in you went straight down to the swings.
*Skidmore*: No, I came to you first. A little girl I was with went to the swings. I went on afterwards.
*Warren*: And left the baby with me.
*Skidmore*: The baby came with us.
*Warren*: But you left him with me. When you have been on the park every night, I have been there haven't I?
*Skidmore*: Yes.

Addressing the bench, Warren now explained to them: 'It was a recognised thing between my wife and myself.' Mr Prynne then asked the girl if Warren had ever asked her to run an errand for him before. She replied that he had.

*Prynne*: When?
*Skidmore*: Not long ago.
*Prynne*: You left the child with him?
*Skidmore*: Yes.
*Prynne*: What was that errand?
*Skidmore*: To fetch Sonny some rock.
*Prynne*: Did he tell you not to hurry that time?
*Skidmore*: No.

In adopting this approach, the accused seems to have been trying to build into his defence the presumption that his killing of the child was not premeditated, and that having sent the girl away on an errand, the idea came to him on the spur of the moment. This was going to be very difficult for him to present, because the indications are from the girl's evidence that by sending her off on previous evenings, he was laying the ground for the one occasion when he wanted not to arouse her suspicions. Also, if the killing were a spur of the moment thing, why, if he had originally intended simply to kill himself, as was stated, and had the means to do so with the laudanum, did he take the razor with him?

Next the court heard from Warren's mother, that on receiving the note, she sent Elizabeth back with a saw as her son had requested; and then from Stanley Hackney in relation to his coming upon the scene of the crime. Here again Warren already had the note written out, indicating that the incident was pre-planned. Dr Moore gave evidence that the cause of James Warren's death was a deep incised wound to the throat which had severed all of the vessels and muscles of the neck to the right side and half of the windpipe down to the vertebrae.

Superintendent Levi Bowley of the County Police now took the stand and related the details of what took place at County Police headquarters. After being interviewed and charged, Warren made a statement in which he said: 'That's it, I can't do anything else but plead guilty. I am straight enough there. I went out with the firm intention to do it at dinner time. I had made a big bet today on Early Hope, running at Haydock Park, and if it lost, of doing myself in. I heard it had lost and went to the park – the Fosse recreation ground – and lay down there and saw my boy Jim with a girl named Edith. I sent her away with a note, as it suddenly struck me I would do away with the child as well with the idea of getting my own back with my wife for taking me to court and losing me my job and disgracing me.'

The statement went on to say that he carried the child to the field. He played with him for about ten minutes and then the child went to him and he cut him with the razor. 'I took the laudanum as soon as I had cut the child's throat, and lay down thinking we should both be found dead together.'

On Friday 23 October, the trial of Arnold Warren was held at the Leicester Assizes before Mr Justice Avory. The prisoner pleaded not guilty. The prosecution team was Messrs C.A. McGurdy MP, and Costello. In Warren's defence was Mr Disney.

Very little new evidence was presented to supplement what had been heard at prior stages of Warren's committal. The story of the accused's previous history, his gambling and domestic problems were all reiterated.

PC Ashburner produced a letter that he had found in the prisoner's clothing when searching him at the time of his arrest, addressed to his old foreman, A. Bolus, at Wilkinson's in Little Holme Street. It read:

Just a last line to you. When you have the misfortune to employ a man who has had a fall, take my tip, don't 'sleer' him over it, for if you had not thrown it at me I should still have been in your employ, but now I am what is called by some men, a wastrel, and in a short time from now, a murderer and a suicide.
Arnold Warren

Apart from trying to shift the blame for his situation to his late employer, the note tends once more to confirm that the killing of the child was not a spur of the moment thing. Unless Warren took pen and paper with him to the scene of the crime, the note was something that he wrote earlier in the day (or possibly even before), and as such, indicates that he intended to kill James before he went to the recreation ground.

Warren was in possession of another letter which was found on him with the one to Bolus. It read:

To whom it may concern,
These are the last words of one who having had the best of chances any man could have, has persistently refused to take advantage of them, and now tells of his last thoughts on looking into his past life – not dreading the future. I know I shall be better off because my life has been one long series of mistakes, independence of master, ignoring my mother's and my wife's advice, and going dead against my parents . . . I have now come to the last of all, a gambler's end, forsaken by my wife and child through my own fault.

The work of the defence, Mr Disney well knew, was going to be a struggle of Herculean proportions. As to the facts of the case, there was nothing that he could dispute. His only option was to convince the jury that at the time he murdered his son, Arnold Warren was mentally unstable.

He drew the jury's attention to evidence given by Mary Warren, that since suffering a bout of typhoid fever some ten years ago, her son had been of an excitable nature. Counsel, he declared, was not so foolish as to say that the prisoner did not take the child's life – but was he fully responsible for his actions when he did so?

In a charge of murder, he proposed, it was usual to look for a motive; however, in this case, no motive could be suggested which would affect a sound mind, and a man who was in such a state of mind that he could not control his actions was insane. If the jury felt that there was any doubt over this, then it was their duty to give the prisoner the benefit of that doubt.

In making this plea, Mr Disney studiously avoided the motive which the accused had himself declared – that he wished to commit the act in order to get even with his wife for making him submit to the indignity and disgrace of being taken to court by her.

His Lordship. Mr Justice Avory, while acknowledging the eloquence of the defence counsel's plea, was not going to allow the jurors to be sidetracked. It was necessary, he told the jury, for him to make plain to them what their duty was under the indictment. If they were satisfied by the evidence that the prisoner wilfully cut the throat of the child, then he was in law guilty of murder. In this case, there was no pretence for saying that there were any circumstances that could reduce the crime to manslaughter.

The defence had invited them to return a verdict that, although the accused cut the child's throat, he was insane at the time. It was not open to them to say, out of mercy to a prisoner, or because they shirked the performance of their duty, that a man was insane simply because it was a convenient escape from the responsibility devolving upon them. The jury must ask themselves whether there was any evidence in this case that the prisoner at the time was suffering any disease of the mind at all so that he did not know the nature and quality of the act he was doing.

In their opinion, he asked, did the prisoner know that he was cutting the child's throat with a razor? If he did not, why had he told the police afterwards that he had cut the child's throat with a razor? Why had he done it? Did he know that he was wrong in doing that?

Finally, it was suggested that there was no motive in this case. The law did not require on a trial for murder that the prosecution should establish the motive with which it was done. The law said that *prima facie*, the killing of one person by another, was murder.

After a retirement of twenty minutes, the jury returned a verdict of guilty. They made a recommendation that as the crime had not long been premeditated, the prisoner should be shown mercy.

Passing the death sentence on the accused, Mr Justice Avory told them that he would forward their recommendation to the proper quarter.

*Leicester Prison, situated on the southern edge of the town. It was here that Arnold Warren was executed on 12 November 1914.*

Arnold Warren was executed at Leicester Prison on 12 November 1914.

PC Ashburner was himself to have a distinguished police career. Joining the Leicester Borough Police (after 1919 becoming the City Police), in May 1912, apart from a period spent in the army from 1917 until the end of the war, he served until January 1946 when he retired as Detective Superintendent.

Superintendent Bowley, as head of the County Detective Department, was in the summer of 1919 to conduct the investigation into the murder at Stoughton of Bella Wright, which has become known more familiarly as the 'Green Bicycle Murder'.

7

# DOES A DYING MAN ALWAYS TELL THE TRUTH?

*Joseph Drury, 1941*

The most difficult types of murder to solve are those where there are no witnesses and the perpetrator has chosen to take their own life along with that of their victim or victims. Evidence such as a suicide note, supposedly detailing their final actions, can also be deliberately misleading. Such appears to be the case in the deaths of Ethel Drury and her daughter Iris Pickering at the hands of Ethel's husband, Joseph William Drury.

Every Monday afternoon at four o'clock, Mrs Minto, the wife of Councillor John Minto, would put on her hat and coat and walk the few yards down the road from her house in Kingswood Avenue to that of her friend and neighbour, Mrs Ethel Drury, in order to 'take tea'.

On Monday 13 October 1941, as part of her regular routine, Mrs Minto knocked on Ethel Drury's door, and was surprised to receive no answer. The house was locked up and silent. Perturbed to find that the daily deliveries of bread and milk were standing uncollected on the front doorstep, she went to see if another neighbour, Mrs Sutton, had any knowledge. Returning to the house together, the two women now noticed a strong smell of gas seeping under the front door, and thoroughly alarmed, sent for Mrs Minto's husband.

A short while after, John Minto and an associate, Graeme Devine, arrived by car, and on peering through the lounge window, spotted the partially-clothed body of a woman behind the settee.

Graeme Devine broke the glass in one of the leaded lights of the front door and the men gained access into the house. Once inside, they found the bodies of forty-eight-year-old Ethel Drury and her twenty-three-year-old daughter Iris Pickering in two of the downstairs rooms – both had injuries to their heads – and Ethel's husband Joseph was dead in the kitchen next to the gas stove which was switched on but unlit, and was the source of the gas that could be smelled outside.

The police were summoned and an examination of the scene was made by Detective Superintendent Harry Ashburner, known for many years as 'Snowy' due to his prematurely white hair.

As no other police officer is referred to anywhere in the evidence given at the subsequent inquest, it has to be assumed that Ashburner (who himself lived nearby on Hinckley Road), decided from the outset that this was, although a tragic incident, an open and shut case.

In the kitchen sink he found a bloodstained screw spanner which was undoubtedly the weapon used to kill Ethel Drury and to render Iris Pickering unconscious. In the lounge was a small safe, the interior of which was bloodstained. Inside were Ethel Drury's lower dentures, indicating that she had been at the open safe when she was struck a violent blow from behind, knocking her teeth out of her mouth and spattering the safe with her blood. The dying woman had then been dragged across the room and laid behind the settee. The killer then forced a gag into her mouth, presumably to stifle any noise that she was still making.

The police surgeon, Dr Neville Spriggs, in his evidence to the coroner, stated that the gag had been removed prior to his examination of the body, something which, as an experienced investigator, the detective superintendent would not have done, so it has to be assumed that it was removed by the killer once he was satisfied that she was dead.

In the dining room, which was the middle room of the house, was the fully clothed body of Iris Pickering. She had three lacerations to her head which also had apparently been inflicted with the spanner. In Dr Spriggs' opinion, these were not of sufficient severity to have killed her. The cause of death was due to a small handkerchief which had been rammed into the back of her throat and another handkerchief tied around her face and mouth which caused her to asphyxiate. In the kitchen, Joseph William Drury lay with his head in the open gas oven, covered by three overcoats, his head supported by some cushions.

An inquest into the deaths was held by the coroner Mr E.G.B. Fowler at the Town Hall on Wednesday 15 October. The coroner was told by neighbours that the Drurys, Ethel and Joseph, were, to all intents and purposes, a happily married couple. He was a wholesale fishmonger who, at forty-two, was six years younger than his wife, and had served in the Royal Navy on minesweepers during the previous war. Although he had apparently been rather concerned recently about the effect on his business of the shortage of fish due to the dangers imposed on trawlers by U-boat activity, he was in general a jovial man and they were 'an ideal couple, absolutely devoted to one another'.

The only voice of dissent was that of John Minto's wife, who, when giving evidence, told the coroner that she and her husband were close friends of the Drurys and that when they visited them on the previous Friday evening, Joseph Drury appeared to be quiet and depressed, something which they had attributed to business difficulties.

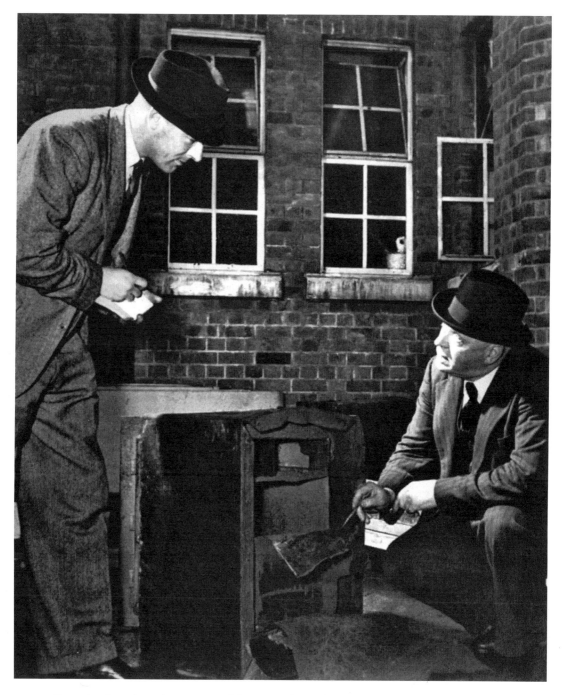

*Detective Superintendent Harry Ashburner (right) and his deputy, Detective Inspector Douglas McMurdo, in this obviously posed picture taken during the Second World War in the parade yard of City Police headquarters. Ashburner joined the Leicester Borough Police in May 1912 and began a distinguished career when, in July 1914, he arrested the murderer Arnold Warren for killing his small son on Western Park Fields (see Chapter 6). He retired in January 1946.*

Iris Pickering was Ethel Drury's daughter from a previous marriage. Iris had married a local man from the Braunstone Estate in 1939, and they had lived in their own home until his call-up for the forces (he was at the time of his wife's murder serving overseas), following which she moved into Kingswood Avenue with her mother and stepfather. She worked as a machinist at the firm of S.D. Stretton in Grange Lane, where she had been employed since she was sixteen, soon after leaving school.

That Joseph Drury killed his wife and her daughter is not in dispute. In addressing the coroner's jury, Mr Fowler told them:

This is a ghastly tragedy. These three people seemed to have been living there on the best of terms. On Monday last, a lady went to keep an appointment there to have tea with them. When she got to the house she noticed a strong smell of gas and after repeated knocking, no one came to the door. Then someone saw someone laying in the front room. The front door was broken open and there in the house were three dead bodies. There was Ethel Drury on the floor in the front room, her death apparently due to a fracture of the skull. In the kitchen was the body of Joseph Drury near the gas oven from which gas was escaping, and his death was apparently due to coal gas poisoning. In the dining room was Mrs Pickering with injuries to her head and also signs of suffocation. Death in this case was probably due to suffocation accelerated by head injuries.

Joseph Drury, having killed the other two, before killing himself, sat down and wrote a letter to me, and to his father-in-law, and in view of these letters it will not be necessary to go into detail in this matter, for in them he makes a complete admission of what he has done.

The coroner then read out the contents of the letter which Drury had left behind for the coroner after he took his own life:

God forgive me, she was a wonderful wife. We have never had a cross word all my life except about that little devil. I cannot write well, my hand is shaking. This is a terrible thing I have done. It started with a row over her daughter.

Unfortunately, due to the original inquest file being closed until 2011, neither this letter nor the one which he wrote to his wife's father are yet available for examination. This is unfortunate because from this point on, the reporting of its contents is paraphrased, and glosses over an important issue – the one that Drury claimed was the catalyst which resulted in him murdering the women. It relates, according to Joseph Drury, to an allegation he made against his stepdaughter and to a resultant threat that he would not have her back again into his house. In the letter, he says that this allegation led to him and Ethel having words, and that he went into the scullery to put a washer on the tap while his wife went to the safe to put some money away. 'I went to her and told her that if she didn't shut up I would hit her. I had a spanner in my hand and before I knew what I was doing I hit her.' The letter then explained that having killed his wife, he waited for her daughter to return home and, 'did the same to her, because it was her that caused it.'

The indications were, Superintendent Ashburner said in evidence, that having murdered his wife, Drury then went upstairs and changed his shirt, which was found in the bathroom. After killing Iris, he once more changed before gassing himself.

George Needham, a jeweller in Southgate Street who was Ethel Drury's father and the recipient of the second letter, addressed simply to 'Pa and May', dismissed its contents saying that having read the allegations made by Drury against Iris, he simply, 'did not believe it'.

This second letter however, carries, in view of the circumstances, an unusual footnote that reads: 'I cannot write any more. You will see what I have written in the other letter. All my affairs are in order, no debts to pay. It is all over Iris. We had a hell of a row over it. I must have been mad to hit Ethel. You know we have been a perfect couple, she was a jewel of a wife. Bury us all together, I will forgive Iris.'

Having heard from the relevant witnesses and read from these two missives, it only remained for the coroner to try to establish an accurate time of death. Dr Spriggs put it as being at least twenty-four hours prior to the discovery of the bodies.

Evelyn Billings, who lived next door to the Drurys, said that during Saturday evening she called around to use their telephone at which time she saw Ethel Drury, but no one else. Later that night, her mother had heard noises which at first she thought were Mrs Billings' baby crying, and then decided it was probably the wireless that she could hear. This effectively puts the time of the murders at somewhere between Saturday night and Sunday afternoon.

Because of the letters left by Joseph Drury, the coroner accepted that he had murdered his wife and stepdaughter before taking his own life, and with the city's most senior detective officer concurring, the matter was closed.

The question which must be asked however, is how truthful was Joseph Drury being in his suicide notes – was he in fact laying a smoke screen?

Until October 2011 – the date when access to the inquest file is arrived at, it is not possible to view the original letters which detail the mysterious allegation that Drury made against his stepdaughter. That she was guilty of such conduct that would cause him to beat his supposedly beloved wife to death with a spanner, and then coldly wait for his stepdaughter to return home in order to first hit her with the same spanner, and then suffocate her with a gag, is stretching credulity.

The day following the newspaper report of the inquest, women from the dead girl's workplace at S.D. Stretton's were so incensed at the innuendo contained in Drury's suicide note that they took the unusual step of contacting the *Leicester Mercury*.

Elected as spokeswoman, Mrs P. Norris of Filbert Street told the *Mercury* reporter: 'I don't believe anyone will believe it for a moment. Iris worked on the next machine to me and I was a close friend of hers. She had been picked out for a ten weeks course in radio location and she had promised to come into the factory to say goodbye on Monday. When she didn't come in I wondered what could have happened.

'She was married shortly before the war and when her husband went out East she gave up her home in which she had been so happy and went to live with her people. She and her mother were devoted. I knew the mother but not the stepfather. Her mother was a lovely woman.

'Iris thought there was no one like her husband. I can hear her now saying, "No one can come up to him." She was young and full of life and went out of course like any other young girl, but if we did not go out together, she always told me where she had been next morning.

'When the girls read the report of the inquest they were most indignant. It upset everyone.'

Two relevant points are brought up here. First the obvious one – that the people who worked with and knew Iris Pickering were sufficiently satisfied that there was no scandal attached to her, and so incensed at what they considered to be lies in the suicide document, they made a public challenge.

Second, however inadvertently, they let it be known that Iris was supposed to be going away a day or so after the murders took place for ten weeks in order to train as an operator in radio location.

Was the dispute in reality between Joseph Drury and Iris Pickering over the fact that Iris was going away on Tuesday for almost three months and Joseph harboured feelings for his stepdaughter that were not reciprocated? This was wartime, and a job working for the War Office in radio location would, after the initial training period, almost inevitably involve the young woman being posted elsewhere in the country to a military or RAF station. With her husband away on active service, was she seeking to aid the war effort and at the same time remove herself from the household?

So far as the actual sequence of events is concerned, those described by the killer were accepted without question: Drury and his wife had a fierce argument, he went into the kitchen, took a spanner, returned and struck his wife who was at the safe, then waited for his stepdaughter and suffocated her.

There are definite question marks here. Because Mrs Billings' mother heard a noise sometime 'during the night', the inference was that the killings took place at night. This is not necessarily so. Dr Spriggs put the time of the deaths as being at least twenty-four hours prior to the bodies being found – i.e. around or before four o'clock Sunday afternoon. Saturday night would put the deaths much earlier than that (as even twelve midnight on Saturday would have been forty hours), and one would expect Neville Ivens Spriggs, who had been the police surgeon since 1913, to have been aware if such a length of time had elapsed.

It was October and 'blackout' would have been imposed quite early in the evening and public transport limited. So if it were Saturday night and Iris (as implied) had been out, she could be expected to have returned home relatively early – well before midnight – thus pushing the time scale further and further back from Dr Spriggs' twenty-four hours.

When John Minto and Graeme Devine looked through the window into the lounge, they saw Ethel's body behind the settee – the curtains were not drawn! Drury is hardly likely to have committed the murders then drawn the curtains back, if for no other reason than that he would have required some light to complete his grisly tasks – among other things, writing the two letters – a fact which would have attracted the attention of the first passing ARP warden. The conclusion has to be that the women were killed not on Saturday night but during Sunday, sometime prior to four o'clock in the afternoon.

Joseph Drury wrote that he and his wife had an argument and he went into the kitchen to mend a leaking tap. He returned to the living room, spanner in hand, and told her that if she didn't shut up he would hit her – which he did.

Again, it would be unusual late at night, in the middle of an argument, to decide to mend a tap washer. In these circumstances, engaged in a fierce argument (as he alleged), it would be more usual for the proponents to be face to face. Why would a half-dressed woman, in the middle of a domestic dispute, decide to put some money in a safe?

The physical evidence at the scene – the bloodstains and dentures found inside the safe – indicate that Ethel Drury was struck unawares from behind, while her attention was focussed on what she was doing in the safe.

Even at this stage, it is reasonable to conclude that Joseph Drury concocted a story to cover his actions. The suicide letter saying that, having first killed his wife, the killer waited patiently, first taking the precaution of changing his bloodstained shirt, for his next victim to return home, was accepted as fact.

In relation to Joseph Drury's version of events, there are several question marks. A supposedly ideal marriage marred by the presence of his stepdaughter, a series of actions which, when examined, are unlikely, and a detailed suicide letter written, despite his assertions of 'a shaking hand', puts the onus of responsibility on Iris Pickering.

If the evidence (such as it is) is examined objectively, there is another possible sequence of events – that it was Iris Pickering, not Ethel Drury who was killed first, which is probably much nearer to the truth.

Instead of occurring on Saturday night, if the tragedy is moved to sometime on Sunday during daylight, this first explains the fact that the curtains – the closing of which after dark under the blackout regulations was mandatory – were open.

Ethel Drury was upstairs, either changing, or more likely, taking a bath. This would ensure her absence from downstairs for a longer period of time and allow her husband to go into the bedroom in order to change his shirt.

If Iris Pickering had gone out and was killed when she returned home – she must have gone somewhere. It would be normal practice for the last person to see her alive to give evidence at the inquest as to the time and place she was last seen. This did not happen – because she did not go out. (Even if she had gone for a walk alone, in the district where she lived, it was unlikely that no one would have seen her.)

Far from being out of the house, Iris was downstairs in the middle room. Taking the opportunity to speak to her alone, Drury was trying to persuade her not to take the job which would involve her leaving, and she, perturbed by his attentions, was refusing. It is very possible that Drury came into the middle room from the kitchen where he was mending the tap, and as such, had the spanner in his hand; alternatively, the argument may have started in the kitchen and moved through into the other room. Losing his temper, he struck her with the spanner, knocking her to the ground, where she lay moaning. Panicking and frightened that his wife upstairs would hear, he stuffed a small handkerchief into the girl's mouth, and then, because that did not suffice to quieten her, took a second larger one and tied it over her mouth.

Realising that he had killed Iris, Drury then decided quite coldly that he would also have to dispose of Ethel. He went quietly upstairs into the bedroom and changed his bloodstained shirt, not putting it in the bathroom until much later because his wife was in there.

Ethel came downstairs in a state of undress (he may even have called her down), and from the kitchen, he asked her to put some money into the safe. Waiting until she had the safe door open and her head near to the opening, he crept up behind and struck her a heavy blow to the back of the head with the spanner – of sufficient force to knock her dentures out and spatter the interior of the safe with blood. When she fell to the ground, he administered further blows to ensure that she was dead.

Drury, needing to write his suicide notes and prepare for his own death, then dragged his wife's body behind the settee in order that it would not be seen by a casual observer, giving him time to compose the letters, muddying the waters. There is no indication of how long after the killings he gassed himself, but this could have been up to several hours later.

At some point, he returned upstairs to once more change, and put the two soiled shirts in the bathroom. Suicides often have a habit before taking their lives of ensuring that everything is neat and tidy. In his letter to George Needham, he says, 'all my affairs are in order, no debts to pay. . .' which may be an indication that irrespective of killing the two women, crimes which he probably committed on impulse, he had, in fact, planned his own death for some time.

In support of those who maintained that Joseph Drury was lying in his final letter to the coroner, he says one very unusual thing in writing to his father-in-law: '*bury us all together.* . .' Surely these are not the words of a man who wishes to go into eternity with a woman he hated sufficiently to commit murder over.

# 8

# 'MOVE IN AGAIN AND I'LL GIVE YOU ANOTHER!'

*George Buxton, 1942*

Life in Leicester during late 1943 was very similar to that in any other city across Great Britain. With the Second World War now moving into its final phase; the Russian army had decimated Hitler's forces in Russia; in Italy Allied troops were slowly forcing the German rearguard action back into southern Europe; and plans for an Allied invasion of Normandy were well under way. On the Home Front, however, things had still not as yet begun to ease. Rationing was very much a fact of life, with food, clothing, household fuel and petrol in short supply. Entertainment was of a basic nature, television was a thing of the future, and most people relied upon radio, the cinema, a drink in the local pub and for some – an evening at the dog track.

Parker Drive Stadium, just off Blackbird Road, was home to the Leicester racetrack, and while providing for many a place to relax and enjoy a small bet on the greyhounds, it also had a more seedy aspect. Race 'fixing' was a common practice, and the petty criminals who ruled the track by fear held sway over much of what happened there.

In December 1942, nineteen-year-old Gordon Arthur Newberry successfully sued the management of the stadium for having been wrongfully dismissed the previous year when he had refused to cooperate in the doping of a dog prior to a race. Consequently, he had later been set up by a kennel lad employed by a gang to make it appear that he had interfered with the result of another race. A few months later, in a separate incident at the end of May 1943, Alfred Clewlow, a thirty-nine-year-old engineering turner, was sentenced to nine months' imprisonment for attempting to bribe a member of the kennel staff to dope a greyhound.

It was in relation to this dubious society that in late 1942, George Buxton, a hosiery worker who lived at 19 Saxby Street, fell foul of one such gang led by Frank Sykes, a general dealer from Martin Street. Sykes, at forty-four, was six years older than Buxton – a widower with no children who had been discharged from the army on medical grounds, and other than the fact that there was a dispute between them over Buxton's association with a woman, the details of their quarrel are not now known. It was sufficient that Frank Sykes decided that Buxton needed to be taught a severe lesson, and set two of his lieutenants, Roland Cleaver and 'Tacker' Smith to deal with the matter. Both of these were 'heavies', responsible for enforcing Sykes' grip on events at the racetrack. Cleaver had not long been released from prison, having served a sentence for black-marketeering.

During the last week in September, Roland Cleaver and some other gang members tracked down their man in the town and gave him a beating. A week later, on the evening of Friday 2 October, George Buxton was in the Nelson public house in Humberstone Gate with a woman by the name of Doris Draycott, whom he had known for several years. Smith, accompanied by some other men, came into the bar, and hoping to avoid trouble, Buxton and his companion decided to leave. In the pub doorway, they were jostled by the men who followed them out into the street where Tacker Smith grabbed hold of Buxton and said, 'We've got you.' Buxton replied, 'Didn't you do enough to me last week.' An airman who was part of the gang then moved in, and flicking their victim's face with his hand said, 'No, we're going to spoil this for you next time.'

Buxton now threatened that he was considering going to the police, to which Smith retorted, 'We're out to do you. We're going to do you properly.'

The men now released Buxton and walked off. A very possible reason for his not being harmed on this occasion was that the dispute had spilled out into Humberstone Gate, which was within yards of the clock tower, an area that on a Friday night would be heavily policed.

Two weeks later, early in the evening of Saturday 17 October after the races were over, George Buxton was outside the dog track talking to an acquaintance, Arthur William Kent, when Smith and Cleaver, along with some of their men (including the airman who was with them at the Nelson), came out of the stadium. Smith called Kent over to him, and when he was within range, swung a punch at him, followed by another. Cleaver shouted that he had got the wrong man and, identifying Buxton, they then all began to chase him down the road in order to inflict another beating.

The following Saturday afternoon 24 October, around five o'clock, George Buxton returned to the stadium for the afternoon's races. This time he had armed himself with a loaded Webley .45 calibre service revolver.

Outside the stadium he encountered Roland Cleaver, with whom he exchanged blows, and getting the better of the encounter, made his way into the stadium and went to the 1s 6d enclosure near to the start, where he knew that he would find Frank Sykes. As Buxton confronted Sykes, Cleaver made an appearance close on his heels, armed with either an iron bar or a bottle. (The enclosure was crowded with people and witnesses were not sure which it was, as after the event it does not appear to have been recovered by the police.) A scuffle broke out and Buxton, breaking away, pulled the revolver out of his pocket saying to Sykes, 'Stand back or you get this!'

Sykes, who was about five paces from Buxton, laughed and went to attack him again, at which point Buxton fired a shot into him. Although he had been hit in the stomach, Sykes said, 'If you can't shoot better than that – throw it away.' George Buxton then fired a second shot and was heard by witnesses to say to the wounded man, 'Move in again and I'll give you another!'

Despite the close proximity of the two men, the second shot had in fact missed its intended target and hit an innocent bystander. Eileen Louvaine Jones, a young married woman, the mother of three children whose husband, a soldier, was away in the Middle East, was standing near to the two men when the incident occurred. It was her first visit to the racetrack. She later told the jury at Buxton's trial that she was in the enclosure watching the racing when she heard an explosion which she thought was the starter's gun going off. There was then the sound of another explosion and feeling pain in her shoulder, she realised that she had been shot. Buxton's second bullet had hit her just above the breast, and lodged in the right side of her back.

At this point, Police Sergeant James Auld and Constable Moore, who were on duty in another part of the stadium, came into the enclosure and saw Buxton pointing the weapon in front of him. While the constable attended to the injured man, Sergeant Auld arrested George Buxton and took him to the track offices where Buxton said to him, 'I done it – I've let him have it. They have been after me over a week.'

Frank Sykes was taken to the Leicester Royal Infirmary where he was examined in the casualty department by Dr Ramsay Liddell, who found that the patient had two gunshot wounds in his abdomen, one on the left side, the other on the right. Buxton's first shot had passed clean through Sykes' body from one side to the other. (In fact, later on, Sykes' wife, while helping him to undress, found the bullet in his clothing.) Typical of the man – full of bravado, Frank Sykes refused medical attention and discharged himself from the hospital – an action that was to cost him his life.

For anyone in this situation, to discharge themselves without being treated is, to say the least, foolhardy, and by late evening, Sykes was extremely ill. The bullet had passed through one of the coils of his intestine, resulting in peritonitis. An ambulance was summoned and he was rushed back into hospital but it was too late. Despite an emergency operation at 4 a.m., the following morning he died. Dr Ramsay Liddell later told the court that had the deceased remained in hospital initially, he would probably have lived.

At Charles Street police station, when interviewed by Detective Inspector William Haywood over the shooting and attempted murder, Buxton told the detective, 'I only had the revolver to frighten him. I didn't intend to murder him. I only wanted to defend myself. I have been attacked several times during the last week.'

*Situated off Blackbird Road,
the Parker Drive stadium in
post-war years became the
Leicester speedway track.
(Courtesy E. Selvidge)*

*Detective*
*Inspector*
*William (Bill)*
*Haywood.*

When later seen again by Inspector Haywood and told that as Sykes was now dead, the charge had become murder, Buxton replied, 'Only that I don't remember any of the shooting.' In relation to the wounding of Mrs Jones, he replied, 'I don't remember the gun being fired at all.'

The trial of George Buxton, which was held during the first week of February 1943 at the Leicester Castle Assizes (the Town Hall Courts not being available), was bizarre, to say the least.

Prior to the trial, the prosecuting counsel, Mr Fitzwalter Butler, and the defence, Messrs Norman Winning and Miles Ward, came to an agreement that if the prosecution reduced the charge of murder to one of manslaughter, then the defence would cooperate and enter a plea of guilty. This in itself is not an unusual state of affairs; in fact, it is common practice where the prosecution feels that their evidence is weak. In this instance, however, such was not the case.

Manslaughter is the crime of killing a human being *without* malice aforethought or in circumstances not amounting to murder. Murder is the unlawful killing of one person by another *with* malice aforethought. Had George Buxton gone unarmed into the stadium, encountered Frank Sykes, and in the course of an ensuing argument, on the spur of the moment, picked up a bottle or some other object and struck Sykes a fatal blow, then that could reasonably be argued to constitute manslaughter.

This, however, was patently not what happened. At some point well before the incident, Buxton acquired for himself a heavy calibre revolver which he loaded with five bullets. He then went to a place where he knew that he would find Sykes. After an altercation with the man, Buxton drew the revolver from his pocket and threatened his victim – 'Stand back or you get this!'

Buxton then deliberately fired a shot into Sykes' body from a range of about five paces. Taunted by Sykes, he fired a second shot which hit Eileen Jones, following this up by saying to the dead man, 'Move in again and I'll give you another!' Having deliberately discharged the weapon twice at his victim, he was preparing to fire for a third time. How much more malice aforethought did the prosecution want?

The judge, Mr Justice Lewis, now entered into the arena, directing the jury to find the accused guilty of manslaughter, which they had little option but to do.

On sentencing Buxton, his Lordship cautioned him with what can only be construed as a degree of levity: 'I would say this, that if I were you I should give up carrying loaded revolvers about. I say no more than that.'

He did, however, go on to say more. His next remark is astounding in the circumstances:

> I consider this [to be a] case in which you shot at Sykes while under extreme provocation. I have heard from your counsel and from the police that there is unfortunately a gang who before this occasion assaulted you. You are a man who has never been in trouble with the police before. One who is described as honest and sober. Long may you continue to bear that reputation.

It is apparent that the person on trial here was not the perpetrator but rather the victim. Frank Sykes was not a man of pristine character, and doubtless lived a lifestyle that sooner or later was going to attract him harm. This, however, does not alter the fact that he died as the direct result of a bullet wound wilfully inflicted by a man who had sought him out with a loaded gun. For all his Lordship's best wishes as to the accused's continuing good reputation, no comment or apparent enquiry was made either by the police or the court as to how he obtained the revolver. Scant attention was paid to the option open to the accused and to any other 'honest and sober' citizen to go to the police and seek help rather than choosing to put himself deliberately in harm's way, taking with him, in the process, a loaded gun. The charge of unlawfully possessing a firearm and ammunition was not proceeded with, so consequently, this matter was never addressed.

In relation to the charge of unlawfully wounding Eileen Jones, who all parties agreed was an innocent bystander, and which was an offence that itself potentially carried a heavy prison sentence, the judge once again displayed inexplicable leniency. On this charge he bound the accused over to be of good behaviour for twelve months in the sum of £5.

Regarding the main charge of manslaughter, Mr Justice Lewis was of the opinion that as George Buxton already spent three months in prison on remand, this was a sufficient sentence, and the accused was allowed to walk from the court a free man.

# 9

# KILLED BY THE MAN SHE BEFRIENDED

*William Cowle, 1944*

Just before two o'clock on a bright May afternoon in 1944, Ivy Laurie Kimberlin had just turned into Springfield Road from London Road with her small son and two other boys when she heard the sound of a woman's screams coming from a passageway nearby. Seconds later, a man came out of the passage, stopped, and turning around, went back out of sight. There was a further scream and she heard the woman shout, 'He has struck me!'

Things then happened rapidly. The man reappeared (Ivy later said that she did not get a look at his face), and ran off along Springfield Road. Next, a young woman, bleeding heavily and holding her hands to her neck, staggered out and collapsed on the pavement in front of her.

The woman was thirty-two-year-old Nora Emily Payne, a clerk at the Petroleum Board offices in Springfield Road, and as in so many instances, her assailant, thirty-one-year-old William Alfred Cowle, was well-known to her.

Born in January 1912, Nora Payne was one of three children, the other two being a brother and a married sister. Prior to working in Springfield Road for the Petroleum Board (formed in 1938 by a coalition of the country's main fuel suppliers such as Anglo-American, National Benzole, S.M. & B.P, the Board was a wartime measure which, under government control, dealt with such things as rationing and the allocation of fuel oils), she had been a clerk at Shell BP House on London Road near to the LMS railway station. It was doubtlessly her experience in this role which had made her suitable for secondment to the Springfield Road office.

During 1941, William Cowle, a painter and decorator who originated from Liverpool, was employed to paint the offices in which Nora Payne worked, and the two of them became friends. Cowle was a strange man, given to fits of melancholy and depression. At his subsequent trial, his mother gave evidence that as a child, and later as a young man, he often suffered with his nerves, experiencing pains in his head, and at such times he would become very emotional and depressed. She also said that from time to time he would disappear from home without explanation, only to turn up working in some

95

*Seen from its junction with London Road, apart from the addition of a modern doctor's surgery on the right-hand side, Springfield Road is little changed from the leafy suburban road that it was on the afternoon that Nora Payne was stabbed to death by William Cowle.*

other part of the country. It is probably fair to say that Nora Payne, a kindly single woman entering her early thirties, identified Cowle as being lonely and isolated and befriended him.

Whatever her intentions were, it is obvious that Cowle quickly became infatuated with her. Throughout 1941, he lived in lodgings in Saxby Street with Nellie May Jones, who described him as someone who 'got on her nerves', being subject to bouts of severe depression, during which he was capable of spending the entire day crying. Sometime towards the end of 1941, he was conscripted into the army for a short period before being discharged as medically unfit in April 1943.

That the two remained in contact during Cowle's short time in the army is apparent because following his discharge, over Easter 1944, he travelled from Norwich, where he was now lodging, to visit Nora at her parents' home in Clarendon Park. Nora's father, Frederick Payne, a retired railway clerk, told the court at Cowle's trial that, 'Every now and again, he used to come to the house.' Mr Payne went on to say that during the Easter holiday, the man came once more to the house to visit his daughter, but he got a feeling that there had been a change in her attitude towards Cowle.

Throughout the period that Nora Payne knew William Cowle, there is no indication that – other than in Cowle's mind – there was ever any sexual relationship between them. It is fairly obvious that she now realised that what had started on her part as a piece of platonic kindness had never been viewed as such by Cowle, and that she needed to end the association. Whatever steps she took in relation to the Easter visit seem to have been completely ignored. If Nora Payne had needed confirmation of the fact that she should do something, it was evidenced in a letter that Cowle wrote to her (which he later alleged was on the day that he killed her), but did not post, which read:

Dearest Nora

Darling, I did enjoy being with you again, even if you were in a bad frame of mind. I am looking forward to June 10th and if all goes well I'll get to Leicester on the Saturday, and if it is nice weather, let us go to Bradgate Park for the day.

I hope that you will try to fix it so that I may see you for a couple of days.

All my love, cheerio, I remain your loving sweetheart.

Following Cowle's visit to her home at Easter, Nora spent some time considering how to end – as kindly as possible – what had become an intolerable situation for her. During early May, she wrote a long and detailed letter which Cowle received at his lodgings in Norwich on Tuesday 16 May. It read:

Dear Bill,

Thanks for your letter card which I received. I am glad to say I am sleeping better now that I had sleeping tablets, but I cannot stand against all the problems that seem to have suddenly come into being. I shall have a breakdown. The only way is to face them and that means being cruel to you.

I only looked upon you as a friend, but you will not take my word as final and that you can make me love you and persuade me to do a thing which my conscience says is wrong.

I appreciate your kindness to me during the past three years but I really feel that the strain of trying to change myself is too much. I know that it is a mean way of telling you on paper, but I have tried so many times to tell you in person, and you will not accept that.

My nature is not to hurt people, but neither of us is getting younger, and I have the right to mix with and meet other men before I decide whom I shall marry.

I want it to be for life, and not an unhappy union that will end in divorce.

I know your impulse will be to come at the weekend – but don't come because I shall be out. I have told mother, and I won't see you if you come.

The letter went on to say that Nora was accepting an invitation to visit London at Whitsun, and that he should not consider visiting her. 'It will be a break and maybe it will ease my mind', she wrote, adding that for her week's holiday, she was going into the country. The letter continued:

> This will be a shock to you, but you must know we can't go on as we have been doing. Be a man, take it the right way and don't think badly of me. If I have broken your dreams, mine are broken too. I will continue to write to you if you want me to.
>
> Remember, I would still like you to get on. . . confide in someone. Don't keep trouble to yourself. Don't brood. Even try to hate me. Before I close, thank you for all you have done for me. It is not my fault that fate plans life a different way. Don't come to Leicester, I shall be cross. More than that I shall not see you.
>
> I just don't know how to end, I have never written a letter like this before, and I hope I never shall again. It is against my nature. I wish you good health and place you in the safe keeping of our heavenly Father.

The day after receiving the letter, William Cowle left his digs at 47 Losinga Crescent, Mile Cross near to Norwich, bought a return ticket to Leicester, and set off to resolve matters in his own way. With him he took a small dagger that he was in the habit of carrying.

Although there was never any confirmation, Cowle maintained when spoken to by Dr Taylor, a prison medical officer, that he saw Nora Payne on the evening of his arrival in Leicester and attempted to talk her into continuing what had become for him their 'relationship'.

Whatever the truth of this may be, on his arrival in the town, he booked in at the Belmont Hotel in Demontfort Street where, the next day, he left his bag before going to find Nora.

As was her habit, Nora Payne left her office in Springfield Road at lunchtime on Thursday and walked to her home at 7 Lytton Road, where she had a meal with her parents before setting off back to work at 1.40 p.m.

It was a twenty minute stroll through Clarendon Park before she was back at the bottom end of Springfield Road, and commenced the short walk up the residential street to her place of work.

How far, or for how long William Cowle had been following her, or as is possible, waiting concealed in one of the secluded driveways up to the houses along the leafy side road, is not now known. (Although reports of the crime talk of a 'passageway', there was not at that time any cut through that could be described as such, and the reference has to be to one of the narrow lengthy alleyways between some of the houses.) As the unsuspecting woman passed the end of one of them, he either came up behind her or leapt from his cover and forced her into the passage. Her startled scream, which first alerted Mrs Kimberlin, probably also frightened him and he first made to leave, and then either changed his mind or regained his resolve, and went back in and stabbed her several times with the dagger, inflicting a fatal wound in her neck, before running away from the scene.

Although help was summoned immediately – Dr John Braithwaite, whose premises were nearby at 7 Springfield Road, rendered first aid, and she was conveyed quickly by ambulance to hospital, Nora Payne died within minutes of being admitted to the Leicester Royal Infirmary.

Having committed the deed, Cowle made his way along London Road and down Mayfield Road into Beckingham Road, where he encountered Constable 198 John Woods. On seeing the policeman, he approached him and said, 'You are a policeman aren't you, I want you to take me to police headquarters – I have just stabbed someone.' PC Woods said Cowle was nervous and shaking, although not in a state of collapse.

On being questioned by the constable as to who it was that he had stabbed, Cowle replied, 'It's a girl – I did it in a fit of temper. . . ' He told the officer that it had taken place in a street beyond Clarendon Park Road, off London Road. The fact that the man was wearing a scarf that was stained with fresh blood and had a smear of blood on his left cheek along with a cut to his left hand, convinced the officer to arrest him.

Interviewed at Charles Street police station by Detective Superintendent Ashburner, Cowle made no attempt to deny the offence. When told that the woman was dead and that he would be charged with her murder, he replied, 'I don't want to say anything except that I am sorry it happened. I had no intention whatever to do it.' He then directed Ashburner to go to the Belmont where he would find behind the clock in the hallway his suitcase, containing the letter he had written but not posted and the one that had brought him to Leicester.

While the facts of the case were never in dispute, William Cowle's state of mind at the time of the murder – to which charge the accused entered a plea of not guilty – was very much a point in issue at his trial before Mr Justice Singleton, which opened at the Nottingham Assizes during the last week of June 1944. The prosecution was conducted for the Crown by Mr W.K. Carter. Mr Arthur Ward and Mr Guy Dixon appeared on behalf of the accused.

Having heard evidence of the events surrounding the commission of the crime, Dr J.L. Merson, a house surgeon at the Leicester Infirmary, gave evidence of admitting the victim to the hospital and the fact that she died within minutes of the admission at 2.25 p.m. Dr Merson later conducted a post-mortem, at which he found that a puncture wound to the neck had penetrated the muscle and entered the trachea. There were also two puncture wounds to the right shoulder and a wound in the back immediately to the right of the spinal column which had penetrated the bone, along with other superficial stab wounds to the woman's back. Death, he stated, was due to shock and haemorrhage following the knife wounds inflicted to the neck and back.

Shown a small home-made dagger that had been recovered from the accused, Dr Merson agreed that the wounds were consistent with those caused by the weapon.

*Having inflicted the fatal wounds on Nora Payne, William Cowle made his way along London Road to Beckingham Road where, encountering PC Woods, he gave himself up to the officer.*

Detective Sergeant Kenneth Springthorpe gave evidence of having recovered a bloodstained Macintosh which was identified as having been worn by Cowle when he stabbed Nora Payne. He told the court that he had recovered the coat from a hedge in Victoria Park Road near to St Mary's Road. (This would indicate that having run off along London Road, Cowle turned left into St Mary's Road, a secluded cut through between London and Victoria Park Roads, in order to divest himself of the bloodstained coat, before returning along Victoria Park Road to Beckingham Road.)

Sergeant Springthorpe gave evidence that during a search of the vicinity, 'I then saw the dagger in the middle of the path in the front garden of no. 5 Springfield Road. It had bloodstains, some of which were not quite dry.'

For the defence, the first witness called was Cowle's mother, Annie May Cowle, who spoke of her son's poor mental state up to the time that he left her home in Liverpool around 1934, which was some time before he engaged in an unsuccessful marriage. The marriage (which had never been ended through divorce), she said, had been an unhappy one and had ended with Cowle being assaulted by a man (presumably with whom his wife was involved).

Mrs Cowle said that it was her son's practice when mentally ill to collect nails and bits of string and other such useless things that he would carry about with him, and that in recent years he had taken to moving about the country from job to job. In answer to a question by the prosecution, she agreed that her son had never actually seen a doctor in order to seek treatment for his depression.

Cowle's brother-in-law, Thomas Myers, a school attendance officer in Liverpool, was the next to be called. He told the court that he had known the accused since 1924 and was married to his sister. He confirmed Annie Cowle's evidence that his brother-in-law was generally regarded as unstable and made a habit of collecting sea shells, string and socks with no feet in them. Speaking of Cowle's habit of disappearing, he said that he was known in the family as 'Wandering Willie'.

From an early stage, it was apparent that rather than fight an impossible battle to deny the events, Mr Ward was going to put them into a context that his client was seriously mentally ill.

His first professional witness was Dr G.W. Taylor, the medical officer at Leicester Prison, who had been observing the prisoner since 19 May, the day after the incident. He told the court that:

> Having regard to what I have seen and heard in conversation I formed the opinion that he [Cowle] was suffering from mental disease on 18 May. He had periods of depression lasting sometimes for three days, and at these times he talked about suicide. There have been other periods of time in between when he seemed comparatively happy. He would say then that he was free from worry, and when I asked him he would say, 'I can't remember anything about it, what is there to worry about.'

Questioned by the prosecution concerning the fact that Cowle had brought the dagger with him from Norwich, Dr Taylor said that Cowle told him that following the assault on him years before, he took to carrying a table knife for protection. After the outbreak of war, with talk of invasion, he substituted this for the dagger which had been made by his brother, and always had it with him.

He was, he told the doctor, in the habit of writing poetry and lengthy letters to his friends. In relation to the incident with which he was charged, the accused said that he remembered having a conversation with Nora which was friendly, but for him an unhappy one (this apparently took place in the passageway), and he remembered hitting her, and then nothing more until he was going down the street holding the bloodstained dagger which he threw away. It was in conversation with the doctor that he mentioned having seen the deceased the evening prior to the murder.

Asked the crucial question, Dr Taylor said that he did not think that when the crime was committed the accused knew the difference between right and wrong, and that in his opinion he was suffering from manic depressive insanity.

Both the prosecution and the judge now asked if he would 'know the nature and quality of the act which he was performing?' To both of them, he gave an unequivocal, 'No.'

The second expert witness brought by the defence was Dr A.N.W. Colahan, who had examined the prisoner on 21 June. His opinion, like that of Dr Taylor, was that Cowle was suffering from manic depression. He concurred that the accused would not, at the time of killing Nora Payne, have known what he was doing, but that the sight of blood on his hands and the dagger that he was holding would, after the act, have brought him back to reality. In conversation with Dr Colahan, Cowle said that the last thing he remembered was kissing the woman, and then seeing her lying on the pavement:

> *Carter*: Did you consider the possibility that this was untrue?
>
> *Colahan*: I accepted his word.
>
> *Carter*: Do you consider the state of his depression was the result of the letter?
>
> *Colahan*: It could have been, but it was more likely to have arisen when he was talking to her – due to the state of finality.

It was now the turn of the prosecution to bring their own expert to give evidence on the accused's state of mind. For this purpose, John Humphrey, the medical officer at Nottingham Prison took the stand. He attested to having examined William Cowle at Leicester Gaol on 9 June, almost two weeks prior to Dr Colahan.

Dr Humphrey, a specialist in borderline mental health, had spent two hours with the accused, and formed a different opinion to the other medical men. He found Cowle to be of average intelligence, although neurotic – the prisoner spent around an hour and a half of the time that they were together in a state of hysteria, which the doctor said was typical of a man in his position. Despite this, Cowle gave him a clear and coherent account of his past life up to and including the day of his arrest.

During his examination, the prisoner was clear about things that he did not disclose at other examinations by Doctors Taylor and Colahan. Cowle recollected seeing his victim at lunchtime, '*when on the way home*', and he gave her a £1 note. (This is significant because it clearly indicates that he approached her twice – once on her way home from work for lunch, and then again later on, when the attack took place.) He also said that when doing this, he moved the dagger, which was in his wallet, to his coat pocket.

Cowle's continuing story as told to the doctor now becomes less plausible. He said that after this, he wrote the note that was found addressed to her. To have done this, he would have had to return to the Belmont Hotel, which was a fifteen minute walk from the route that he would have taken if he had accompanied the woman on her way to lunch, written the note, placed it in his baggage at the hotel, and then made the return journey to intercept her on the way back to work. While the timescales are such that it is just possible for him to have done this, it is unlikely. Also, he told Dr Humphrey that in the conversation he had with Nora, she told him that, 'his people did not come up to the social standard of her people.' In view of the sensitive nature of the letter that Nora Payne wrote to Cowle, this latter assertion is unlikely (a view obliquely expressed by the judge). If such a thought were in her mind, it is far more likely that she would have included it in the letter. It was after this point that Cowle maintained that he had no further recollection of what had happened.

Dr Humphrey was of the opinion – one diametrically opposed to that of Doctors Taylor and Colahan – that while the accused was neurotic, he was not suffering from any mental disease which would prevent him from knowing what he was doing when he killed Nora Payne.

It now came to the point where the judge, in his summing up, needed to give the jury guidance in reaching their decision. He began by pointing out to them that it was not the course of events that resulted in the killing that was in dispute, rather the state of the prisoner's mind at the time. Referring to the letter sent by the deceased which provided the catalyst for the incident, he made the comment, 'I cannot help thinking that you will come to the conclusion that never was a more decent or proper letter written.'

The summing up was succinct and objective:

'On 16th May the accused received that letter at Norwich and came to Leicester. They [the jury] had not heard what he did on 17th May beyond what they had heard from one doctor, to whom the accused said he had seen the girl that evening. One could not help wondering when told that the sight of blood might have brought back the accused's memory, whether the scream of a woman might equally have brought his memory back.

'The evidence that they had heard was that there had been two screams and in the interval between them the man seen by Mrs Kimberlin had come out of and returned into the entry. They had heard that when the accused met Constable Woods he was shaking nervously, but not collapsed. Whether he was a nervous man, a normal man, or an extraordinary man might he not be shaking then?

'They might consider whether the expression on social standards would be used by the writer of the letter he had read. If she did so it might well be that it would cause annoyance.

'Did they consider that the accused was suffering from such a defect of reason through disease of the mind as not to know he was stabbing the girl? If they thought that was shown, their verdict would be guilty but insane. On the other hand, if they thought that was not so, they would not add those words.'

Having retired, the jury were absent for only fifty-five minutes before returning a verdict of 'Guilty'.

The clerk to the court asked the foreman, 'Have you no words to add to that one word?' The foreman said, 'No Sir.'

Sentenced to death, Cowle lodged an appeal on the grounds that misdirection at his trial by Mr Justice Singleton had negated his plea of insanity. On 24 July, Mr Justice Humphreys for the Court of Criminal Appeal, dismissed the application.

*Now a busy suburban street, in 1944, Lytton Road was a quiet backwater. Nora Payne
lived at no. 7, near to Queen's Road.*

The summing up of the Appeal Court was that the case made on his
[Cowle's] behalf that he was insane at the time of his actions had been very
properly considered at the trial, including the accused's previous history of
peculiarities. The summing up by the trial judge was a model which could not
be properly criticised at any point, and the correct conclusion – that William
Cowle was sane – had been reached. (Mr Justice Humphreys did, however,
add the rider that, 'in dismissing this appeal, we think it only right to say that
we would take the view that no one would probably have been surprised if
the jury had returned a verdict of guilty but insane.')

William Alfred Cowle was hanged at Leicester Prison on 8 August 1944.
The execution was slightly unusual in the fact that it was a double hanging.
The sentence was carried out at the same time as William Frederick George
Meffen, aged fifty-two, who was sentenced to death for the murder of his
stepdaughter, Winifred Ellen Stanley at their home address in Derby in
February 1944.

# 10

# TO STOP A WOMAN'S COMPLAINING TONGUE

## *Darshan Singh, 1957*

Soon after 6.20 a.m., on the morning of Wednesday 18 September 1957, a telephone call was received at Leicester City Police headquarters from a man who stated that while travelling into work on the top deck of a Corporation bus, he had seen what appeared to be a body lying in the small area of grassland just off Walnut Street, known as Grasmere Park. Responding to the call, Police Constable Green was sent to make a check of the park, where, at about 7.30 a.m., he found the body of an auburn-haired woman wearing a grey raincoat with a black collar over a blue and white print dress, lying near to a flowerbed; she had been strangled.

The area was sealed off and a team of detectives under the head of the CID, Detective Superintendent Eric Lacy, began a murder investigation. The woman was quickly identified as Joyce Stanton, of 44 West Street, a thirty-year-old divorcee. While a search was conducted of the park and surrounding area for the dead woman's shoes and stockings which were missing (other than this the body was fully clothed), the Home Office pathologist Dr E.M. Ward attended, and having made a cursory examination, arranged for the body to be removed to the mortuary. People living in the immediate vicinity, when questioned, told the police that they had heard nothing unusual during the night and there were no signs of a struggle on the wet ground where the deceased was found, and little attempt had been made of concealment; all of which led the detectives to the conclusion that the woman had not been killed at the spot where she was discovered. Although the park was secured at 7.25 p.m. the night before, the gate and surrounding hedge were only just over 3ft high, and it would have been an easy matter for the killer to have heaved the body over from the road into the flowerbed where it was spotted by the bus passenger once it was daylight.

The autopsy conducted by Dr Ward showed that death had been caused by manual strangulation sometime around midnight the previous evening. There

was a mark at the base of the neck which had been caused by a blow, and there were two bruises on the chin, all three of which had been inflicted while she was still alive.

In the meantime, the woman's missing high-heeled, peep-toe shoes were found a short distance away from the scene of the crime, neatly placed outside the front door of a house at 94 Filbert Street. The occupant of the address, an Asian by the name of Avtar Singh, was interviewed by the police and denied all knowledge as to how they came to be there, and he said that he did not know the deceased.

Joyce Stanton was born in 1927 as Joyce Lay. One of five children, as a child she had lived with her parents nearby at 41 Outram Street and attended Narborough Road Girls School. Married at the age of eighteen to Frederick Stanton in 1945, she had two children who lived with their father, after the marriage ended in divorce in 1955. Since then, she had been living at several addresses across the city with a Sikh two years younger than herself named Darshan Singh, who was employed as a labourer.

Within less than a year of the birth of their first child in late 1956, things began to fall apart. Joyce, through her relationship with Darshan Singh,

Seen from the air during the 1980s, Grasmere Park is in the centre of the picture to the left of the City Football Club. Napier and Raglan Streets have been removed to make way for the growing Leicester Royal Infirmary complex and St Andrew's housing estate. The spot where Joyce Stanton's body was found is marked with an 'x' (centre left). (Courtesy G. Fenn)

associated mainly with Indian men who, like her partner, were single and very much isolated from female company in what was, at that time, essentially a white community. Consequently, she was receiving a lot of attention to which she did not seem to be averse.

By December 1957, only a month or so after her first child with Singh was born, Joyce Stanton fell pregnant again. Towards the end of her pregnancy, while they were living at the back of the police station in St George Street, Joyce wrote a note to a friend, Elizabeth Iwasiuk who, until recently, had been a neighbour, prior to moving to the Saffron Lane Estate. As a result, the two women met in the Rainbow and Dove public house on Charles Street near to where Stanton and Singh were living. Joyce wanted to leave Darshan Singh, who, while they were talking, came into the premises and told her that he wanted to speak to her outside. At first she refused but he then told her that the baby was crying and needed attention so she went with him. Obviously worried, Mrs Iwasiuk waited about ten minutes and then followed them out into the yard. She heard Joyce say, 'Darshan I'm finished', to which he replied, 'You finish with me Joyce, and I'll finish you!'.

*The Rainbow & Dove public house where, in December 1957, Elizabeth Iwasiuk overheard Darshan Singh say to Joyce Stanton, 'You finish with me Joyce, and I'll finish you!' (Courtesy E.R. Welford)*

Realising that they were no longer alone, he told Mrs Iwasiuk to go back to her old address in nearby Baker Street (the *Leicester Mercury* building now stands on the site) and get a carrier bag of clothes which Joyce had asked her friend to look after for her. Mrs Iwasiuk asked the other woman if that was what she wanted, and receiving no answer, decided that she would do so. Once she had fetched the bag, Darshan Singh took it from her and both he and Stanton left.

It is obvious that although the couple now moved from St George Street into a house at 46 Napier Street which they shared with other Indians, things deteriorated rapidly. A second child was born on 13 August, and on leaving hospital, instead of returning home to Napier Street, Stanton moved into lodgings at 44 West Street. A week later, accompanied by her father Alfred Lay, she went to Napier Street to collect the remainder of her clothes, indicating that so far as she was concerned, the break was final.

On his return home from work just before six o'clock on the evening of Tuesday 17 September, Darshan Singh found a court officer waiting at the house, who served on him an Affiliation Order relating to the two children that Joyce Stanton had borne, citing him as the father. With only a limited knowledge of English, Singh took the document to the house of another Indian, Shri Dara who lived around the corner at 2 Raglan Street, where Dara's landlady Mrs Smith explained to him the content of the order.

From this point on, Darshan Singh's story and the evidence are in direct conflict. Following the discovery of the body, during the afternoon of 18 September, Singh was arrested by Detective Superintendent Lacy and taken to Charles Street police station where he was interviewed.

Singh's story was that after being served with the order, he walked round to see Shri Dara in Raglan Street. He remained there a short while, and after listening to some Indian music, left the house at eight fifteen, returning to 46 Napier Street where he went straight to bed and slept until the following morning.

That he was lying was proved by the statements of several witnesses who saw him during the evening in the vicinity of the deceased's lodgings and later in her company in a public house.

At half past eight, a man named Stanley Bird, a male nurse, was approached by Darshan Singh in West Street. He showed him the summons and asked for directions to no. 44. Although Bird had never seen Singh before, he picked him out the following day in an identity parade.

Joyce Stanton was having supper with Janice Nixon, one of the other occupants at 44 West Street, when Singh arrived at the house, and leaving her meal, she went down to answer the door to him. A short time later Mrs Nixon saw the two of them talking on the doorstep.

Stanton appears now to have agreed to go for a drink with Singh and discuss the implications of the court order which she had obtained against him. The couple walked together across the Welford Road recreation ground to Granby Halls and along Aylestone Road to the Cattle Market Hotel.

The licensee of the Cattle Market, Wilfred Cartwright, who knew the accused as a regular visitor, and two customers, Annie Kilmartin who lived in Chestnut Street, and Annie Taylor from Filbert Street, all gave evidence that the couple were in the pub from around half past eight until they left together at 9.45 p.m. The two women said that Stanton appeared to have been crying.

After she walked out of the Cattle Market Hotel into Aylestone Road, Joyce Stanton was not seen alive again. Where she and Darshan Singh spent the next two hours prior to her death remains a mystery.

Darshan Singh, a slim, clean-shaven young man, was interviewed at length through an interpreter by Eric Lacy. He had, he told the detective, been living with Stanton since her divorce two years previously, and that they had lodged at several addresses – including, significantly, 94 Filbert Street, which was the house where her shoes had been found. Singh went on to say that he had known the occupant, Avtar Singh since June 1954, and that while living in Filbert Street, Joyce had been involved in affairs with several other Indian men, including Avtar Singh. As a result of these liaisons, Singh said the two of them had quarrelled and he had on two occasions been beaten up by a group of Indian men, once in Napier Street and once outside of the Granby Halls.

Lacy asked the accused if the beatings were over Joyce, to which Singh replied that they were, and that her allegations that he was the father of her children were untrue because she was having sex with other men while she was living with him.

Darshan Singh now began to tell the blatant lies which were to be his downfall. Asked by the detective superintendent if he had seen Joyce the previous night, Singh replied, 'No, I didn't see her three weeks.' On the last occasion that he had seen her, he said, she told him that when things were sorted out about the children, she would be glad to leave him, and that she was going to live with Avtar Singh. She told him, 'When the court proceedings are over and I have left you the children I will go to Avtar . . . a lot of Indians love me, when I have left you I shall be happy always. . . ', to which he said he had replied, 'I shall be very happy when you have left me.'

When further questioned, he persisted with his story that he had not seen Joyce for three weeks, that he had returned to his house from Raglan Street and had not gone out again, and was asleep by 8.45 p.m. (the time at which he was actually seen by Janice Nixon talking to Joyce on the doorstep of her lodgings), and even maintained that he did not know where West Street was.

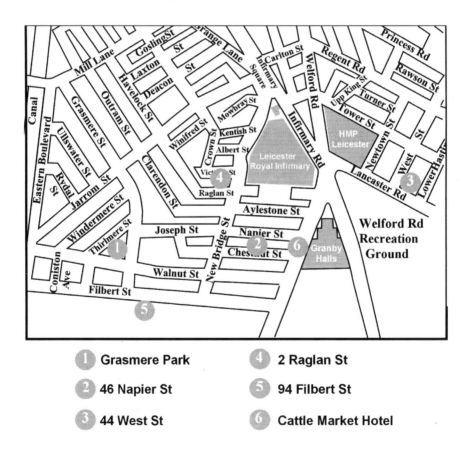

| | | | |
|---|---|---|---|
| 1 | Grasmere Park | 4 | 2 Raglan St |
| 2 | 46 Napier St | 5 | 94 Filbert St |
| 3 | 44 West St | 6 | Cattle Market Hotel |

*Aylestone Road and Granby Halls area. The addresses in Napier and Raglan Streets have since been demolished to make way for extensions to the Leicester Royal Infirmary.*

Superintendent Lacy put it to him that he had been identified as the man who went to 44 West Street and was seen talking with the deceased. Singh replied, 'I don't know where she lived. She went from me taking her clothes with her. She said she was going to her father and mother. I last saw her three weeks ago when she came out of hospital.' Asked if he was angry or annoyed when he was served with the Affiliation Order, Darshan Singh replied, 'No, it not hurt me in any way because when I have seen her she was going to do this thing.'

After being charged on 20 September with the murder of Joyce Stanton, the accused replied, 'I have nothing to say, I never saw her that day.'

The trial of Darshan Singh opened two months later on Monday 18 November at the Nottingham Assizes before Mr Justice Oliver. The barrister for the prosecution, Mr W.A. Fearnley-Whittingstall QC, shrewdly avoided attempting to prove that Singh had murdered Joyce Stanton in a fit of anger over her taking out the court order against him. He chose to go down the road that the prisoner had made a calculated decision that it was time to resolve matters by removing the woman once and for all from his life. In his opening address, Mr Fearnley-Whittingstall told the jury, 'Here is a prisoner who in his mind you may think had a motive for removing this woman's complaining tongue. . . '

The prosecution then proceeded to lay before the jury the circumstances of the prisoner's association with the deceased and his persistent denials, despite independent evidence to the contrary, that he had not seen her on the night of her death. Emphasis was placed on the damning conversation overheard by Elizabeth Iwasiuk: 'You finish with me Joyce, and I'll finish you!'

In respect of the visit to 44 West Street, Mr Fearnley-Whittingstall commented, 'It is quite clear that he was seeking her out – and had found her – in respect of the complaint that she had made.' There was good reason for this assertion. At one point during the police interviews, Darshan Singh told Detective Superintendent Lacy, 'She said to me, when the Court proceedings are over and I have left you the children, I will be single. . . '

Throughout the proceedings, Fearnley-Whittingstall carefully avoided alleging that the defendant had, in a fit of temper, gone to the dead woman's lodgings and, having tried later to reason with her in the pub, killed her on the spur of the moment in an act of desperation. This would have first required him to prove the accused's state of mind at the time the act was committed, and had he successfully done so, given the defence a clear opportunity to gain the jury's sympathy. After all, from the indications as to Joyce Stanton's state of mind, it was her intention that having successfully placed responsibility for their two small children on the prisoner, she would abandon them and regain her freedom.

Making a crucial point, Mr Fearnley-Whittingstall brought to the jury's attention the statement made by Darshan Singh concerning Stanton's intention to leave him, 'When the Court proceedings are over and I have left you the children I will go to Avtar, a lot of Indians love me, when I have left you I shall be happy always. . . ' When, asked the QC, was this said to him? What court proceedings? The only court proceedings which Stanton had taken were related to the Affiliation Order – which had been served on the accused just hours before the woman was murdered – yet the prisoner maintained that he had not seen or spoken to her for three weeks.

The prosecution now dealt with another issue, that of Avtar Singh – the third party in what was rapidly developing into a somewhat sordid triangle in which the victim, while certainly not deserving to die for her frailties, was herself emerging as being less than beyond reproach.

Avtar Singh lived at 94 Filbert Street, at whose front door Joyce Stanton's shoes had been placed. (Although a question mark was initially raised over the fact that her stockings also appeared to be missing, there is in fact no evidence to show that she was wearing stockings at the time of her death.) Initially, while admitting to being an acquaintance of Darshan Singh for three years, and to the fact that he was aware that the accused was known to be living with an English woman, he somewhat foolishly (especially as the couple had lodged with him at one point), denied knowing or having ever seen Joyce Stanton. Questioned by the defence about his alleged association with her, he replied, 'I have never seen her, and I don't know her.' When asked to account for his whereabouts on the evening of Tuesday 17 September, Avtar Singh told the jury that he got home from work about 8.30 p.m., had a meal, and was in bed by half past nine. In the absence of any evidence to the contrary, this was accepted by the court.

Above and opposite: *Fifty years on, Grasmere Park is now set out formally as a children's play area. Some of the original Swedish whitebeam trees remain, as does the low boundary hedge.*

Forensic evidence in relation to certain aspects of the case was now presented to the jury. First, grass cuttings taken from Darshan Singh's trouser turn-ups, and from a washing copper containing soapy water at 46 Napier Street, were found to be similar to those growing on Grasmere Park. Superintendent Lacy had also recovered in Darshan Singh's bedroom some leaves from a comparatively rare Swedish whitebeam tree. Evidence was given by James Watson of the Parks Department that between thirty-six and forty such trees were planted in the Grasmere Street park along with a similar number along Fosse Road, and three in Abbey Park. While initially appearing to be quite an impacting piece of evidence linking the accused to the place where the body was found, its relevance was in reality, theatrical. The accused lived within walking distance of the park, it was September and the onset of autumn and he could have picked up leaves from the trees on his shoes at any time while in the immediate area. In fact, he does not at any time appear to have been asked if he had ever been in the vicinity of the park, in which case, only a denial would have been relevant. Secondly, red fibres were found on the dead woman's mackintosh and cardigan which matched a similar fibre found on clothing belonging to Avtar Singh.

For the defence, Mr G.R. Swanwick opened his examination of Avtar Singh by saying, 'It is not part of my duty to accuse you of anything but from eight fifteen until eleven forty-five, were you alone in your house?' The witness replied, 'Yes.' 'No other witnesses?' 'No.'

Clearly Mr Swanwick was seeking to muddy the waters, so in relation to the fibres found on Joyce Stanton's clothing, his next question, 'Did you know that a piece of red wool from her clothes was found on your jacket?' was to be expected. Avtar Singh replied, 'I did not see it and know nothing about it.' The defence then asked, 'If such a piece of wool was found can you say where it came from?' The witness replied, 'I have never worn this coat for some considerable time, but I have a red jacket from which it might have come.' While not contributing to the immediate case against Darshan Singh, this evidence did conclusively show that Avtar Singh was also lying to the court in his denials of knowing Joyce Stanton.

It is apparent that in relation to the contest between the prosecution and the defence, it was the prosecution who held the better cards. W.A. Fearnley-Whittingstall followed a clearly defined path – the accused had killed Joyce Stanton as part of a premeditated plan in order to prevent her from leaving him with two children to bring up, the parentage of whom he disputed, while she went off to resume the life of a single woman.

The defence barrister, Mr G.R. Swanwick, unfortunately proved to be both at a disadvantage with his client, whose credibility had been effectively destroyed, and somewhat inept at convincing the jury that the whole case against his client was based on circumstantial evidence. He himself called no evidence in support of the defence.

Other than a weak attempt to throw suspicion for the killing on Avtar Singh (it was hardly likely that having murdered the woman he would have placed her shoes on his own doorstep), and proving that the witness was lying when he denied being involved with Joyce Stanton, Mr Swanwick was struggling to extricate his client. At one point, he made a desperate attempt to cast doubt on the veracity of the evidence of the witnesses (one of whom, the landlord of the Cattle Market, Wilfred Cartwright, actually knew Darshan Singh), who gave evidence of the sightings during the evening, as to whether it was the accused who was seen in West Street and with the victim in the Cattle Market Hotel, stating that this was a pivotal question.

He then went on to postulate that, despite the fact that the victim was very short (being only 5ft tall), it would have been almost physically impossible for Darshan Singh – himself slightly built – to have taken the woman back to 46 Napier Street and kill her, as doing so would have probably caused some commotion that would have alerted the other occupants of the house, and then carry her 'sagging body' through the streets to the park where it was found.

To say that this attempt to confuse the issue was weak is an understatement. While it was agreed by both sides that Stanton was not killed exactly where

*The newly-built development and attendant car park of the Leicester Royal Infirmary are on the ground previously occupied by the house at 46 Napier Street and the Cattle Market Hotel on Aylestone Road. (Courtesy E.R. Welford)*

she was found – because of the lack of traces on the damp ground of the parkland and flowerbed – it was never established where she was actually murdered. Neither the prosecution, nor anyone else for that matter, ever suggested that she had been taken back to the house in Napier Street after leaving the pub. It was highly possible that wherever the couple spent the two hours between leaving the Cattle Market pub and Joyce Stanton being murdered, around midnight, Darshan Singh deliberately walked her along Walnut Street, and on reaching the vicinity of the park, ensuring that there was nobody about, he could have struck the blows that were found on her neck and chin, knocking her to the ground before strangling her. It would have been a simple matter then to simply tip the body over the hedge into the flowerbed just inside the park. The whole incident would have been over in a matter of seconds. The removal of her shoes and placement of them outside Avtar Singh's house was a premeditated attempt to make it look as if the woman had gone into the house prior to her death, first removing her shoes and leaving them outside the door as was customary.

The result was virtually a forgone conclusion. After a two-day hearing, the jury of ten men and two women retired for a little over an hour before returning a verdict of guilty. Darshan Singh was sentenced to life imprisonment.

The conviction against Darshan Singh on purely circumstantial evidence was made possible through his own stupid lies. The fact that he had been seen by several people in company with Joyce Stanton during the evening prior to her death, both at West Street and later in the Cattle Market Hotel, made his insistence that he was at home in bed – alone – patently untrue. Had he gone along with what the witnesses all told the court, and conceded that he was with the woman from 8.45 p.m. in West Street until leaving the pub on Aylestone Road at 9.45 p.m., his story would have been totally credible. If he then said that they parted company and he returned home, not knowing where she went after she left him, it would have been an impossible task for the prosecution to put a case together. As his defence pointed out to the jury – the fact that he was with Joyce during the three quarters of an hour prior to her death, 'does not lead you to within three miles of proving murder'. As it turned out, with the defence that was presented, which was an obvious fabrication, the prosecution's job was made relatively easy.

## 11

# 'HE HAD BEEN A BIT CHEEKY TO ME'

### Roy Riddington, 1957

When the newly-built police station was opened at the junction of Welford and Houlditch Road in September 1957 as the headquarters of Leicester City Police's newly-created 'B' Division, no one could have imagined that within a few weeks, the first major incident to be dealt with there would be the tragic murder of a young child who lived nearby.

Eight-year-old Keith Frederick Priestley was the only child of Kenneth Priestley, a Midland Red bus driver and his wife who lived at 106 Heather Road. Keith was a pupil at Knighton Fields Road West Junior School, and at the weekend attended Sunday school in the nearby church rooms. On Thursday 10 October 1957, Keith returned home from school, and after drinking a cup of tea, about a quarter to five went out, as was his habit, to play in front of his house.

A short while after, his grandfather Jack Richardson saw the boy playing happily with a ball. 'I was outside getting some coal when Keith ran down the path and threw his ball on the garden. . . I looked up and he was gone.' The boy was playing normally and Mr Richardson assumed that he had simply moved out of sight. At a quarter past six when Keith's mother went to fetch him in because she had not seen him since her return home from work, he was no longer there.

Puzzled at his disappearance, and assuming that he had simply wandered off, she and her husband began to look for the child, searching the local streets and visiting the homes of neighbours with whom they were friendly to see if he was watching television with one of them. At eight o'clock, now thoroughly alarmed, the worried parents went to the police station, five minutes walk away at Houlditch Road, to report their son missing.

Roy Riddington was a twenty-three-year-old unemployed man who lived with his mother at 150 Knighton Fields Road East. A well spoken, ex-grammar school boy, Riddington was a misfit. Despite having the benefit of a good education, he was unable to hold down a job and had no friends. His abiding interest was music, and having been a member of the local church choir since boyhood, he was now the church organist. He was also a teacher at the Sunday school that Keith Priestley attended.

A tall, fair haired young man with a slightly stooped gait, always dressed, winter or summer, in a fawn coloured Macintosh, he bore a strong resemblance to the later television character, Frank Spencer. (Having grown up and later worked in the area, the author was familiar with Roy Riddington as a local figure, and speaks here from personal recollection.)

About the same time that Keith Priestley went out to play, Roy Riddington also set off from his home in Knighton Fields Road East and walked the hundred or so yards up Burns Street into Heather Road where the boy was playing. Whatever pretext he used to entice the child away – without Keith first checking with his grandfather – will never be known, but at five o'clock, the two of them were seen a matter of yards away from Keith's house at the junction of Heather Road and Scott Street, by fifteen-year-old Brian Crookes, who lived nearby.

The man now began to take Keith Priestley on a circuitous tour of the adjacent streets. Half an hour later, at five thirty, Brian Crookes and his brother Roger again saw the pair walking hand-in-hand back down Heather Road from the direction of Welford Road, but before reaching Keith's home, they turned off left into Sutton Road towards Knighton Lane East.

*Roy Riddington lived on Knighton Fields Road East, within a five minute walk of Keith Priestley's home on Heather Road.*

*Having first walked Keith Priestley along Knighton Lane East in the direction of Welford Road, near to Sir Jonathan North Girls School, Riddington turned around and was seen taking him towards Seven Bridges.*

Between 5.30 p.m. and 5.45 p.m., they were twice spotted by witnesses in Knighton Lane East, first by a man named Butler, near to Sir Jonathan North Girls School, and then heading in the opposite direction by Mrs Margaret Pratt, going towards Seven Bridges.

They were next sighted three quarters of an hour later by a man who had known Roy Riddington for some fifteen years. Norman Jackson, who lived on the same road as Riddington at no. 111, was cycling along University Road around twenty minutes past six when, on stopping at the traffic lights at the junction of University and Welford Road, he noticed his neighbour. 'He had a little boy with him', he later told the Leicester magistrates, 'and was holding his hand. I saw them cross University Road to the corner of the cemetery, and then to the big gates at the entrance to Freemen's Common.'

It is apparent that having enticed Keith away from home, Riddington first walked with him down Scott Street into Knighton Fields Road East. It could have been in his mind to take the child back to his own house but he changed his mind. He then took him along Welford Road and back down Heather Road before turning into Sutton Road. It is pure speculation, but in going back almost to Keith's front door, Riddington, having not gone to his own house with the boy, could have decided to return him home. (At this point, while his parents would have been annoyed at him for going off with the man, because the child knew Riddington from Sunday school, their suspicions as to an ulterior motive would probably not have been aroused.) But at the last moment, he once again changed his mind and diverted down onto Knighton Lane East.

On Knighton Lane East, Riddington seems to have become indecisive. First he turned left up towards the school, and then stopped, and retracing his steps, took the boy down to the Seven Bridges, past the recreation ground to Saffron Lane.

At this late stage of an October afternoon, daylight would now have been failing, and with the onset of dusk, Roy Riddington must have known that very soon, if not already, Keith's parents would be looking for him. He now made a decision that in view of this, he needed to get the boy away from the area where he was known. In order to be in the Freemen's Common area by twenty past six, he would most probably have taken the child a short way along Saffron Lane and then up Knighton Fields Road East, past Keith's school and the swimming baths, under the railway bridge and up the hill. Logically at this stage, *once more passing his own house,* he would have turned off down Kingsley Street into Oakland Road and then left onto Welford Road, well away from where the lad was known.

Roy Riddington was definitely not bright by any standards. The fact that he was known locally by so many people, and was openly walking around the area of both of their homes for some considerable time, in full view, does not seem to have entered into his calculations. What is with hindsight unfortunate, is the fact that none of the people who knew him to be strange and saw him leading a small boy by the hand in the late evening, with darkness falling, challenged him.

By the time they arrived at the junction of University Road, they had travelled a considerable distance, and the eight-year-old must by now have been very tired. The pair spent some time on Freemen's Common, either for Riddington to allow the child to rest or possibly while he turned over in his mind, if he had not already decided on a location, where he intended to kill the boy. (The common itself was a warren of allotments with an accompanying railway line.)

About seven o'clock, some two hours after he had abducted Keith Priestley and forty minutes after being seen by Norman Jackson, Roy Riddington was seen with him one final time by James Larn, who lived at 4 Main Road, Freemen's Common. Larn was out on the common when he heard what he described as a scuffling noise. Shining his torch, he saw in its beam what he later described as, 'A tall fellow with a young lad on the main pathway over the common. They were walking towards Aylestone Road, they were walking fast, the man looked back over his shoulder more than once.' In fairness to Larn, he had no valid reason to be suspicious. The pathway over the common was a well used cut through and it was still early evening, and he did not know either Riddington or the boy and he could have been looking at a father and son, or elder and younger brother taking a shortcut over the allotments.

Keith's parents, frantic with worry, were now making their way to the police station, where once the report had been taken, soon after eight o'clock, a full scale search was initiated. Sadly it was too late, as around the time that officers were being called in and the search begun, Roy Riddington was safely back at home, and Keith Priestley was already dead.

*Seen here in 1953 as an inspector, Robert McCrory was in 1957 the commanding officer at the newly-opened Welford Road police station and led the search for Keith Priestley.*

*Detective Sergeant*
*Edward (Ted) Ward.*

An incident room was set up at Welford Road police station under the direction of Detective Superintendent Eric Lacy, while the uniform divisional commander, Superintendent Robert McCrory took control of the ground search. Over fifty officers were moved into the immediate vicinity, and along with neighbours, the search, hampered now by total darkness, began in earnest.

Early the following morning, enquiries had effectively split in two directions. Detectives were interviewing everyone who might be able to supply information as to sightings of Keith, while McCrory's men were conducting a physical search of the area.

With news of the sighting by Norman Jackson, the emphasis switched immediately to Freemen's Common, and once James Larn had come forward with his information, the search became centred there. In a somewhat unusual move, in order to expedite matters, an approach was made to the Wyggeston Boys School, situated opposite the common, and the second and third years of the sixth form were released from their studies to assist in searching the wells and allotments on the common for the missing child.

Meanwhile, with a rapidly growing picture from witnesses of the sightings in and around the Welford Road area of the boy and his abductor, by Friday mid-morning, a hunt had begun for Roy Riddington.

At 11.35 a.m., Detective Sergeant Edward (Ted) Ward saw Riddington in Lower Hill Street near to the Employment Exchange in the town centre. Approaching him, the sergeant told Riddington that he wanted to ask him some questions about his movements the previous afternoon and evening. Riddington immediately went onto the offensive, telling the detective, 'You have no right to question me. I have done nothing wrong. How do I know you are a police officer – where is your warrant card?' Knowing that he had got his man, Ted Ward showed the suspect his warrant card and resumed his questioning concerning the man's movements the previous evening. In answer to him, Riddington replied, 'I was at home, if you think I had anything to do with that little boy that is missing you are wrong – I never saw him.'

Duly arrested he was taken to Welford Road police station where under interview, Riddington told Sergeant Ward, 'I was with Keith Priestley last night but I left him on the corner of Sutton Road and Knighton Lane East.' Not satisfied with his answers, the sergeant continued to question the suspect and after a while, Riddington said to him, 'If I tell you the truth will it help me? He is in the water by the Old Mill at Aylestone. We went for a walk by the canal, and as he had been a bit cheeky to me at Sunday school, I thought I would teach him a lesson. Something came over me and I decided to push him in the water. As I pushed him in he said, "What did you do that for?" When I left him, the back of his head was sticking out of the water. I am sorry for what I have done now.'

With this admission, having first notified Detective Superintendent Lacy, Ward went with Riddington to the canal at Aylestone where, along with other officers, he met the CID head. As described by Roy Riddington, they found the child's body in the water. Dr E.M. Ward, the pathologist, certified the cause of death as drowning.

Eric Lacy now took over the interview process back at the police station, where Riddington said to him, 'Can you help me? I need some help.' Asked by the superintendent what he meant, the prisoner said to him, 'Well you see, I am backward in some things, but in others I am good. I appreciate good music – I play the piano and the organ. I read a lot and am keen on the church, in fact I was a Sunday school teacher. But unfortunately, I cannot keep a job. It's my nerves, so I don't want you to take advantage of me.' When later charged with the murder of Keith Priestley, he replied, 'I can't believe it. I don't know what on earth made me do such a thing.'

The bulk of the prosecution evidence was heard on 31 October by the Leicester magistrates. Having listened to the witnesses who attested to having seen Roy Riddington with the child during the relevant times, he was committed in custody for trial at the next Assizes.

*Opened only a few months prior to the disappearance of Keith Priestley, it was to the new police station at the corner of Welford and Houlditch Road that Roy Riddington was taken for interview following his arrest.*

Riddington's trial, which lasted for only two and a half hours before Mr Justice Paull, was held on Monday 3 February 1958 and centred primarily around the accused's mental condition.

Superintendent Lacy, the final witness for the prosecution told the jury that Riddington had, among other things, said to him, 'I only intended to teach him a lesson. I was lured, I am afraid by the river. I still can't believe it, what made me do such a thing?'

Lacy also told the court that during his remand while awaiting trial, the accused man had written two letters to him, saying that he had not intended to kill the boy. In one he said that he was full of remorse and asked for fairness at his trial, saying that, 'On the night in question I was not myself, my mind was really distracted.'

He also wrote in the letters that not everything that he had said on interview was correct, and that he had 'manufactured' some of the things in his statements. 'One [thing that was] made up,' he wrote, 'was when it was suggested to me that the boy said something when he went in, I said [that] he said, "What did you do that for?" That is untrue.' He also said that after the deed he was, 'in a state of terrible emotion and panic struck', and that after trying to get help he became

124

panicky and went home. Evidentially the letters held little to influence the result of the trial, and in relation to his assertion that he had tried to obtain help, there is nothing whatsoever to substantiate this claim.

During his interviews with Detective Superintendent Lacy, however, one interesting point emerges. Having visited the scene of the crime, Lacy, a detective with almost twenty-seven years service behind him, had the depth of the canal measured at the point where the lad met his death. The body was found 13ft from the bank – almost in the middle of the canal. At this point, the water was 3ft 10in deep. Less than the boy's own height, the superintendent pointed out to the court. Toward the bank the water became progressively shallower.

While being questioned, Roy Riddington told Lacy that after pushing Keith into the water, 'he made an effort to get the boy out and got wet doing so.' This is quite important in two respects. First, although it was not given in the course of the prosecution evidence, it was obviously with a view to covering this statement by the accused that Eric Lacy had the depth of the canal measured, and then pointed out that at 3ft 10in, it was not as deep as the boys' height at its deepest point. Had the boy merely been pushed in, he could have easily climbed back out. Therefore, the only reason for Riddington to enter the water himself would have been to push the child under.

Secondly, if he were telling the truth and did enter the water – when Roy Riddington returned home at around eight o'clock that night, his shoes and clothing would still have been wet, a fact that could not have been overlooked by whoever was at the house on his return.

Mr A.M. Lyons for the defence elected not to address the jury on behalf of his client and opted rather to bring medical evidence as to the accused's state of mind. During his time spent in remand, the prisoner had been held at two separate gaols, Leicester and Birmingham, in order to allow independent medical assessments to be made.

The first witness called by Mr Lyons was Dr Percy Coates, the senior medical officer at Birmingham Prison. He told the court that during his interviews with Riddington, 'He was apathetic, indifferent, and showed no emotional reaction to his position. When discussing the offence alleged against him he showed no remorse of any sort.'

Dr Coates' assessment was that Roy Riddington was mentally ill and suffered from schizophrenia. Questioned by the judge, the doctor told him, 'It is highly probable that when he committed the act he was insane.' Mr Justice Paull asked, 'Would that bring him within the legal definition of insane?' Dr Coates replied, 'Yes.'

Next to take the stand was Dr George Grayling, who had made observations on Riddington at Leicester Prison. He told the jury, 'His intelligence could be regarded as low average, in spite of the fact that he attended a Grammar School.' He concurred with Dr Coates' opinion that the accused was schizophrenic.

Again the judge posed what had now become the central question. 'Is it your opinion that at the time he committed this offence – if he did it – he was insane?' Without hesitation, Dr Grayling confirmed that such was his opinion.

The jury found Riddington guilty without retiring. On consigning the prisoner to a secure mental institution for the criminally insane, Mr Justice Paull told them that, 'Riddington would be taken away and looked after so there would be no possibility of anything happening again.'

# 12

# 'SHE TOOK MY ANNIE AWAY FROM ME'

About half past eight on the morning of Saturday 27 August 1960, Wilfred Bates was working in the butcher's shop which he managed on Fosse Road North opposite the Fosse cinema, when a woman burst into the shop screaming that a man had forced his way into a house nearby and she needed help. Running to the house a few doors away at 180 Fosse Road North, Bates went in through the front door, the glass panel of which had been smashed, and into the passage just in time to see the figure of a man with his back to him disappearing into the rear room. As the man escaped through the kitchen door, the butcher went after him and saw the bloodstained body of a woman lying on a settee in the sitting room. The incident was the culmination of a stormy domestic dispute that had begun a few weeks earlier.

Adolfas Rastenis, a forty-six-year-old Lithuanian who was employed as a celluloid dipper, came to England at the end of the Second World War. At that time, in 1945–6, the British government, desperate to rebuild the country's labour force in the aftermath of the war, sent representatives to the refugee camps across Europe and recruited men and women to come to this country to become European Volunteer Workers, of which Rastenis, as a displaced person, was one.

In 1957, he met Annie Violetta Toone, who was already married, and the two of them began an affair. A short while after, in 1958, they moved in together and lived at a number of addresses around Leicester. In August 1960 – by which time Rastenis had taken the name Adolf Toone – they were living at 26 Highfield Street.

Annie Toone had worked at Corah's hosiery factory in Burley's Way for some time prior to settling down with Adolfas Rastenis, and in 1956 became friendly with a middle-aged spinster, sixty-five-year-old Ida May Spradbury, who also worked at the factory as a lace cutter. Ida Spradbury, a single woman, had lived for the last twenty years with her mother at 180 Fosse Road North. Not long after the two women became acquainted, Ida's mother died and she continued to live there alone.

In March 1960, Annie Toone left Corah's, but continued her friendship with Ida Spradbury, and during the summer holidays that year, the two of them took a break together during the first week of August at the seaside holiday resort of Skegness. It was after this holiday that things deteriorated between Mrs Toone and her lover Adolfas.

On the day after their return, Sunday 6 August, Annie Toone told Rastenis that she was leaving him as she had met another man at Skegness who she intended to marry. Rastenis was devastated by the news, and over the following days, a running dispute developed between them, with the Lithuanian trying to persuade her to stay with him – although as Annie later told the court at his trial, he had no intention of them ever being anything other than common-law partners, having told her that 'he would never marry an English woman'.

On Thursday 10 August, following a quarrel, Rastenis beat Annie up, revealing for the first time a violent side to his nature. This sealed matters as far as she was concerned, and she made plans to move out of their Highfield Street lodgings for good. At the end of that week, she took what clothes she could carry and moved in with Ida Spradbury at 180 Fosse Road North.

It seems to be from this point that Rastenis evinced a dislike for Ida Spradbury which quickly developed into a hatred sufficient to motivate him to kill her. The question is why? At a later time he told the police that, 'She took my Annie away from me. . . ' and that 'she spoiled my life. . . '

Logically, the focus of his emotions should have been either Annie Toone or the man for whom she had left him. It therefore has to be assumed that Ida Spradbury played a bigger part in their break-up than actually came out in evidence. Intriguingly, nothing other than the fact that his surname was Rilett is known about this 'other man'. The presumption that Toone met Rilett for the first time in Skegness, and in the space of a week had a whirlwind romance, on the strength of which she decided to forsake her current partner in order to marry him, is, to say the least, naïve. So the question has to be asked, had, unbeknown to the Lithuanian, a liaison between the two existed for some time, and the holiday with Miss Spradbury was arranged as a cover for them to spend some time together? Did Adolfas Rastenis realise that Ida Spradbury had been party to concealing a long-term affair? Whatever the truth, from the time that Annie Toone moved out of their lodgings, Adolfas Rastenis placed the blame for his misfortunes squarely on Ida Spradbury.

Sometime between Annie moving out of Highfield Street and Thursday 25 August, Rastenis – obviously aware that she had moved in with her friend – went round to Fosse Road North with some clothing that Annie had left behind and apologised for hitting her. Shaking hands, he took his leave, as she thought, for good.

However, so far as Adolfas Rastenis was concerned, the matter was far from over, and around seven o'clock on the evening of Friday 26 August, he appeared on the front doorstep of 180 Fosse Road North. Thinking that he had come to say a final goodbye, Annie Toone let him in, but it was soon apparent that this was not so. Rastenis became agitated and argumentative, and it took the two women some time to calm him down. Eventually, after making him some tea, they persuaded him to leave.

The Lithuanian now attempted to drown his sorrows in the local hostelries, and four hours later, around 11 p.m., he turned up once more in an extremely drunken state. Refusing to allow him entry, Toone sent him away to sleep it off. Unable to go far in his drunken condition, Rastenis collapsed on the pavement nearby and shortly after was arrested by the police for being drunk and incapable.

He was taken to Charles Street police station where, in accordance with age old practice, he was put into a cell overnight to sleep it off. At seven o'clock the following morning, the charge sergeant, satisfied that the prisoner was now sober and fit to understand what was happening, charged him with the offence of being unlawfully drunk in a public place and bailed him to appear on the following Monday morning at Leicester City Magistrates Court.

*Adolfas Rastenis and Annie Toone lived in a flat at 26 Highfields Street, before Annie moved out to live with Ida Spradbury.*

An important factor here is that having been searched by the police before being locked up, there can be no doubt that when he left the police station soon after 7 a.m. on Saturday morning, Rastenis was not in possession of any kind of weapon.

A little over an hour later, Annie Toone and Ida Spradbury were at the house on Fosse Road North when they heard a ring at the front door bell. Guessing that it was the Lithuanian, Annie told Miss Spradbury, who was in the kitchen at the time, not to answer it. Ignoring her, Ida Spradbury went to the front door.

What happened next is described by Annie Toone in her evidence at Rastenis' trial. 'I told her not to open it because I knew who it was,' she told the court. 'Next I heard a sound of breaking glass. I dashed out to get help. When I came back there was a collection of people in the kitchen and I saw Miss Spradbury laying on the couch.'

*The old Charles Street police station building, where Adolfas Rastenis spent the night prior to murdering Ida Spradbury. The station has since been acquired for development. (Marks can be seen either side of the gates where the large plaques with the old City Police emblems have been removed.)*

On hearing the door glass being smashed, Annie Toone ran down the road and into Gubbin's butcher's shop to summon Wilfred Bates, who went back with her to the house. Entering through the open front door, Bates briefly saw the figure of a man in the passage, and then going through to the rear of the house, he found Ida Spradbury lying on a settee with multiple stab wounds, apparently dead.

Leaving the flat, Bates went into Battenburg Road in time to see Rastenis, who had escaped through the back gate into an alley which gave out onto Battenburg Road, running away towards Mantle Road. He gave chase, calling to passers-by to assist him. He was joined by another butcher, a young lad who was working at a delivery van. (Abandoning the chase, Bates now returned to the house to see if he could he could do anything for Ida Spradbury.)

131

*Ida Spradbury lived for twenty years on Fosse Road North near to the corner of Battenburg Road, opposite the Fosse cinema.*

*Adolfas Rastenis escaped through the back door of 180 Fosse Road North into Battenburg Road through this alleyway at the back of the houses, where he was spotted and chased by Wilfred Bates.*

Peter Reginald Jacques, a leading mechanical engineer in the Royal Navy, who had just returned a few days earlier with his family to their home at 53 Paget Street from a tour of duty in Malta, was walking along Paget Road when he heard people shouting and saw Rastenis, bloodstained and carrying in his right hand the knife with which he had stabbed Spradbury, being chased by the butcher's boy. Jacques grabbed Rastenis, and after a fierce struggle, the sailor managed to knock the knife from his hand and kick it away from them along the street. Holding onto the man, he was now joined by Thomas Baker, a post office engineer from Tetuan Road, and having secured the Lithuanian, they sent the butcher's boy off to get assistance.

In a slightly bizarre turn of events, having detained Rastenis and calmed him down somewhat, Thomas Baker now offered the man a cigarette 'because he looked ill'. Baker and Jacques found that they had not got any matches to light it for him, so leaving him with Thomas Baker, Peter Jacques went into a nearby shop to get some matches. Looking out of the shop window, he saw that taking advantage of the situation, Rastenis was again putting up a fight and had broken away from Baker.

The pair gave chase once more, and as Thomas Baker grabbed Rastenis for a second time, the killer reached into his pocket and attempted to pull something out. Overpowering him, Baker found that he had been trying to defend himself with a coal hammer. This time they held on firmly until the police arrived and arrested Rastenis.

Adolfas Rastenis made his first court appearance before a packed public gallery two days later at Leicester City Magistrates Court where Detective Superintendent Eric Lacy made an application for his remand in custody for one week. Unshaven, wearing a dark grey suit and open-neck shirt, when asked by the chairman of the magistrates, Mr Cyril Hadley, if he wished to apply for legal aid, Rastenis did not appear to understand the question, and it became obvious that with a very limited knowledge of the English language, any further proceedings would have to be conducted through an interpreter. (At the request of Superintendent Lacy, the charge pending against the accused in relation to the drunkenness offence the day prior to the murder was adjourned *sine die*.)

At the remand hearing before the magistrates on Friday 16 September, Rastenis, through an interpreter, entered a plea of 'not guilty' to the murder of Ida Spradbury. Mr Hutchison, for the prosecution, outlined to the court the background to the killing and the events immediately leading up to it.

When interviewed at Charles Street police station, Mr Hutchison told the court that Rastenis told detectives, 'I lost my temper because she took my Annie away from me.' Significantly, he alleged that when Ida Spradbury came to the door on the fateful morning, it was she who was holding the knife, and that he became enraged by her by calling him, 'a bloody foreigner', the result being that he took the knife from her and stabbed her to death.

This assertion is fundamentally flawed. Annie Toone identified the knife with which her friend was killed as belonging to Adolfas Rastenis. It was one which, during the two years they lived together, she told the court, he habitually used to cut up his food.

*Detective Superintendent Eric Lacy.*

When Rastenis was arrested on the Friday night, he was thoroughly searched before being put into the drunk cell to sleep himself sober. At that time he had no weapons in his possession, and consequently left the police station without any. His lodgings at 26 Highfield Street were a fifteen minute walk from the police station. It is safe to assume that although no one saw him do so, he returned home, collected his knife and pocketed the hammer (which was brand new), before making his way across the town to Fosse Road North. His possession of the coal hammer is a matter for speculation. Having armed himself with the knife it is unlikely that he took the hammer as a weapon of attack. More probably, he envisaged difficulty in gaining access to the flat and proposed to use it to force an entry – which he apparently did.

Dr Ernest Milford Ward, senior pathologist at the Leicester Royal Infirmary, gave evidence that when he performed a post-mortem examination of the body of Ida Spradbury, the woman had sustained eleven stab wounds, of which the fatal one had pierced her left kidney and severed the main blood vessel to the leg. Later, during the subsequent high court trial, he gave the opinion that the wounds were inflicted by someone in a frenzy – in the case of the mortal wound, he said, the knife appeared to have been driven in to the hilt.

The trial of Adolfas Rastenis opened at the Leicester Assizes before Mr Justice Havers during the last week of October 1960.

Prosecuting, Mr R.K. Brown opened by telling the jury that the accused was mentally 'a very sick man'. 'Therefore,' he told them, 'You will find inevitably in this case that your enquiries will be concentrated [on] and largely concerned with, the state of this man's mental condition.'

Rastenis claimed, said Mr Brown, that after being bailed from the police station on the morning of the murder, he went to 180 Fosse Road North where, in his own words, 'Annie's friend came to the door with a knife in her hand, I say I want to see Annie'. He maintained that as he pushed against the door, he broke the glass with his elbow. She called him a 'bloody foreigner', and 'I lost my temper and took the knife from her. I stabbed her a lot because I lost my temper. I think it is all her fault, she took Annie from me. She break my life I lost everything.'

Whether the glass was broken as he described, or whether Ida Spradbury, refusing him entry, managed to momentarily shut the door against him and he smashed the panel with the hammer, is not known. In view of Annie Toone positively identifying the knife as belonging to Rastenis, that he is lying – certainly in part – in his version of the events that took place at the door, is certain.

Between the date of the murder and the trial, Annie Toone married the man for whom she had left Rastenis – and who for all intents was the root cause of the domestic dispute. When she gave evidence, it was under the name of Annie Violetta Rillet, now living at an address in Grantham. In respect of Mr Rillet, other than that he was a figure in the background and a catalyst to Annie leaving Rastenis, nothing further was said to the court in the way of background concerning him.

In giving her evidence, slightly built and wearing glasses, Annie, with little emotion, told the court that Rastenis took the news that she was going to leave him and get married very badly. 'He thrashed me,' she said, 'and I had to seek police protection.' Perhaps with a touch of irony, having told the jury of his declared intention never to marry an English woman, she added, 'I was fond of him. There were certain things about him that appealed to me. He was kind and I wanted to be kind to him. I didn't think he would be upset about me leaving him.'

The defence counsel, Mr J.A. Grieves QC, also took the line that Rastenis was mentally unstable, and elected to mitigate for his client's actions and ask the jury to find him guilty, not of murder, but of manslaughter on the grounds of diminished responsibility. 'There is no dispute that the tragic death of this woman was caused by the hand of this man,' he readily conceded.

Called by the defence to give expert evidence, Dr James O'Riley said that he considered the prisoner to be certifiably unsound of mind, suffering from depression, and that at the time of the killing, 'his responsibility was substantially diminished'.

On Wednesday 26 October, after retiring for three hours, the jury found Adolfas Rastenis guilty of the manslaughter of Ida May Spradbury on the grounds of diminished responsibility. In sentencing him, Mr Justice Havers told Rastenis, 'In view of the medical evidence that you are now certifiably of unsound mind, my proper course of action is to sentence you to prison for life.'

# 13

# 'YOU'RE DEAD NOW BILL'

## *John Crosbie, 1966*

'Midnight Murder Brawl – Scot Stabbed In Leicester Street!' This, accompanied by a photograph of a detective talking to a householder at the door of a terraced house, was the *Leicester Mercury* headline on Saturday 16 October 1966.

The leader continued, 'A Scotsman died after a stabbing incident in Elm Street off Humberstone Road, Leicester, shortly before midnight last night.' In fact, this was the story of a sordid incident which brought home the truth of the old adage, 'when thieves fall out', and in truly Glaswegian style, on this occasion when thieves fell out, one of those involved met a violent and brutal end.

The dead man was William Johnstone, a twenty-six-year-old plasterer from Glasgow who had lived in Leicester for some years and was known among his associates, because of his raucous sense of humour, as the 'Joker'. Since the second week in September, he had shared a flat at the rear of a shop at 134 Humberstone Road with two other Scotsmen, John Ritchie and a man named McDowall.

His assailant was a twenty-one-year-old fellow Glaswegian by the name of John Lyons Crosbie, who lived nearby at 45 Larch Street. Coming to Leicester while still a schoolboy in 1959, he had already acquired an impressive criminal record with convictions for theft, housebreaking, assault, malicious damage, office breaking and robbery.

Along with John Crosbie's thirty-four-year-old brother, Henry Black Crosbie, and an associate, Thomas (Tommy) Taylor, the men formed part of a loose group which frequented local public houses. John Crosbie and Bill Johnstone had known each other since the middle of that summer, having met up some time in July – prior to Johnstone's moving in with Ritchie – and it was a few weeks after this that a rift occurred among them.

During the first week of October 1966, the flat at 134 Humberstone Road was the subject of a police raid, when detectives arrived to conduct a search for stolen property. Although nothing incriminating was found, it was apparent to the three occupants that the arrival of the 'polis' was not by accident, and that someone had pointed a finger in their direction. Through their own process of elimination – helped by the fact that the night prior to the raid John Crosbie had been seen going into Charles Street police station – they arrived at the conclusion that he was the person who had informed on them, and from that point a running feud developed, with the group splitting into two camps; Johnstone, Ritchie and McDowall on one side; and the Crosbie brothers and Tommy Taylor on the other.

Matters came to a head on Thursday 13 October. John Crosbie went alone into a Working Men's club near to his home and was unfortunate enough to run into Ritchie, McDowall and Johnstone who were in there drinking. Making a quick exit, he made his way further along Humberstone Road to the Albert Hotel. When he came out of there a short while later, the three were waiting outside for him.

According to Crosbie, Bill Johnstone said to him, 'It is about time you and me had a square Johnny, instead of all this messing about.'

Realising that he was seriously outnumbered, Crosbie told them that he did not want any trouble, and walked off. He returned home to 45 Larch Street, and a short while later, the front window was smashed. Grabbing a poker from the fire grate, he opened the front door and was confronted once more by the three men.

Crosbie, when later interviewed by the police, alleged that Johnstone, who was armed with a knife, stepped forward to attack him, and in self defence, he hit him in the eye with the poker before slamming the door shut. There now ensued a great deal of shouting and banging on the door before his would-be assailants left.

At his trial, John Crosbie told the court that the following evening, in fear of a renewed attack, he returned home early using a circuitous route and entered the house through the back way. Later, he and his brother, along with Taylor, went into the town drinking.

They returned to Larch Street by taxi at the end of their evening out, around eleven o'clock, and on paying off the driver, saw that John Ritchie was standing at the corner of Larch and Elm Street. Ritchie walked over to them and said, 'Billy is around the corner, and he wants to sort it out – now.' Looking into Elm Street, they saw Johnstone standing in the middle of the road.

At this point, according to Crosbie, leaving his brother and Tom Taylor in the road with Ritchie, he went into 45 Larch Street. 'I went into the house and got a sheath knife and an airgun. I took them because I was frightened.'

Having armed himself, he went back out, prepared for a confrontation. 'I went out again and past the bottom of Elm Street. Billy Johnstone was still standing there. He beckoned me and said, "Come on Mug."'

Crosbie now said that he returned into the house, accompanied by Taylor and left again by the back door (climbing over a wall), and decided to make his way to Humberstone Road. Instead, inadvertently taking the wrong direction, he emerged in Elm Street. There he saw his brother Henry and Tommy Taylor fighting with Johnstone.

*With the redevelopment of the area, the houses at the end of Larch Street where John Crosbie lived have now disappeared, to be replaced by modern flats.*

At this point it is worth pausing to examine Crosbie's version of events. Certainly the fact that Johnstone and Ritchie were waiting for the others to return home indicates that some sort of showdown was planned. In a situation where numbers counted, where was McDowall? The most logical answer is that he was aware of what he could be getting into – the Crosbies had a fearsome reputation – and that he simply (and sensibly) decided that he wanted no further part.

If Crosbie is to be believed, the situation was somewhat reminiscent of a Western 'main street shoot-out'. John Ritchie, the messenger, Billy Johnstone standing waiting in the middle of the road . . .

If this was the scenario, what now happened to Ritchie? He does not figure anywhere in the events which followed. Did he naively leave the scene thinking that having issued the alleged challenge, Henry Crosbie and Tom Taylor would also withdraw, leaving it to the two protagonists to settle matters on their own, or did he realise, as is more likely, that things were getting out of hand, and opt for flight rather than fight?

The fact is that when John Crosbie re-emerged, armed with a 9in sheath knife, his brother and Tom Taylor were in the middle of the road struggling with his intended victim, who was now alone. Again, the question must be asked – with John Ritchie having left Johnstone to his own devices – did

Johnstone, now realising the peril that he was in, also attempt to run, and were Henry Crosbie and Tommy Taylor preventing him from doing so until Henry's brother got back to them to finish matters?

Finally, John Crosbie was no stranger to the district in which he lived. For him to say that he went over the back wall of his house into an alleyway which he thought would bring him onto Humberstone Road is nonsense. He had to know that it came out into Elm Street, exactly where his intended victim was being held.

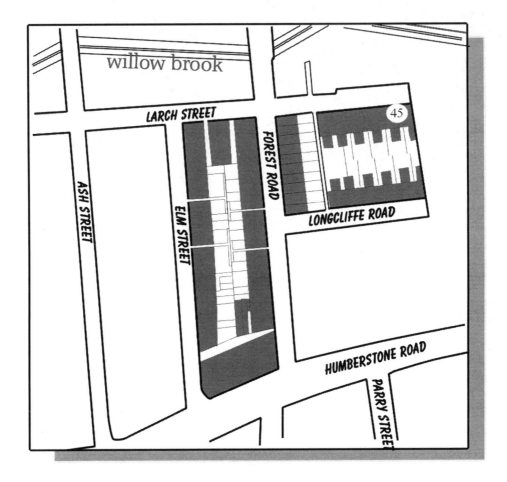

*The layout of this area has altered since 1966 through the development of new housing. Elm Street has gone and there is a small green recreation ground at the corner of Forest Road and Larch Street. From the plan it can be seen that by going over the garden walls from the rear of 45 Larch Street, John Crosbie could access the passageway cutting through from Larch Street to Longcliffe Road. Opposite the corner of Longcliffe Road and Forest Road, he then had a choice of two entries that went to the back of the houses in Forest Road which ran either way in a 'T' across the backyards of two houses. By taking one of these and climbing over the dividing wall, he could easily access a further entry going onto Elm Street. The whole process would have taken him less than five minutes.*

John Crosbie continued with his story. Emerging from the alleyway and seeing the struggle taking place, he pulled the sheath knife from his belt, and Johnstone, breaking away from the melée, came towards him – he also had a knife in his belt. Crosbie said:

> It was the first thing I looked for. He came towards me, slow and determined, a walk like a lion's walk, as if he were going to eat me. I could not run away from him because he would have caught me. I remember a small struggle, and then he was sitting across the front of my legs on top of me, and twisting my bad leg. I struck out, I may have been stabbing, I don't know. He had his hand going in his trousers for his knife. I was doing my best to get up, but he had a knife in his left hand stabbing down towards my stomach. He was leaning over me, and blood was coming out of his mouth. He fell off, and I walked down the road.

At this point, Crosbie said, he still had the airgun in his belt and the knife in his hand. After the incident he said that he walked back home and put the knife and gun in the 'kiddies' box. In this he was lying. The knife was recovered the next day by police from a drain in Larch Street. Crosbie told the court, 'I did not know at this point that I had killed Johnstone. I had no intention of killing him. I thought he was going to kill me. I had no alternative in what I did – I did not want to do it.'

The story as told by John Lyons Crosbie was, however, in several points at variance with that told by independent witnesses, which unfolded at his trial.

That John and Henry Crosbie, along with Tommy Taylor, spent the evening of Friday 14 October drinking in Leicester city centre, and then returned home by taxi is no doubt true. That John Ritchie was waiting for them at this point is definitely in issue. It would appear that the three of them went out again after being dropped off, and the encounter with Ritchie actually occurred a little later on.

About eleven o'clock that night (the time when John Crosbie maintained that they were dropped off by the taxi), a group of five youths were in Larch Street near to its junction with Ash Street, opposite to the fish and chip shop. John William Woods, who lived at 47 Ash Street, was with his brother David and three other lads. The group were engaged in a deal of horseplay when the two Crosbies and Taylor came up the road towards them. (It is feasible that after being brought back by the taxi, they made for the nearby fish and chip shop.)

One of the youths, David Gilbert, a bricklayer who also lived in Ash Street, said that one of the men asked them what was going on. Obviously intimidated (the lads, being local, most likely knew the Scotsmen by sight and reputation), Gilbert told them that nothing was 'going on', they had been having a bit of a fight, and it was all over. One of the three then took out a small gun and hit John Woods across the eye with it. Before leaving them,

Henry Crosbie smiled at the injured lad and said, 'The fight's not over until there's blood about and the ambulance has been.'

About 11.15 p.m., people in Elm Street were awakened from their sleep by the sounds of shouting and fighting, and looking from their windows, witnessed the fatal attack. (One neighbour told a newspaper reporter the following morning, 'It's not unusual for people to be fighting around here, but last night there was more noise than usual. . . ')

A prime witness was Brenda Studd, a married woman who lived at 56 Elm Street. Looking out of her bedroom window, she saw Henry Black Crosbie and Tommy Taylor struggling with Johnstone. John Crosbie came from the nearby passageway with a knife in his hand. He ran across the road saying, 'I'll knife you!'

A strange thing then occurred. John Crosbie, at this point, appears to have lost all self control, and lashing out indiscriminately at anything or anyone in his path, first stabbed Tommy Taylor in the stomach and then his brother in the chest. This unexpected turn of events gave Johnstone a moment's respite, and breaking away, he attempted to run off down the road, but Crosbie overtook him within a few paces and after a short struggle, took him down to the ground. The grappling continued in the gutter, and then managing to get on top of Johnstone (not, as he alleged, the other way round), Crosbie was seen to stab his victim several times with the sheath knife. Satisfied with his work, Johnstone now got up and, standing next to the dying man, was heard to say, 'You're dead now Bill.'

Walking across to his injured brother, he said to him, 'I've got him this time pal – he's dead.' (He does not at this stage appear to have been conscious of the injuries that he had inflicted on his brother and Taylor.) About to leave the scene, Crosbie now realised that Mrs Studd had witnessed the murder, and holding up the knife to her, called, 'You will get this if you say anything to the police!'

With the arrival of the police and medical assistance, the injured were removed from the scene (Billy Johnstone died in the ambulance en route to hospital), and a murder enquiry was set up.

The following morning, with teams of detectives led by Detective Chief Inspector Norman Cox combing the area for evidence and taking witness statements, it was not long before John Crosbie was in custody. He was charged with the murder of William Johnstone, and causing grievous bodily harm to his brother, Henry Black Crosbie, and Thomas Taylor. Along with Taylor and Henry Crosbie, he was also charged, 'that they did go armed so as to cause fear and unlawfully did fight and make an affray.'

The trial of John Lyons Crosbie took place the following month at the Leicester Assizes. On Friday 25 November, after four days of hearing evidence, the jury retired after lunch and returned a verdict of guilty on all of the charges. In respect of the wounding charges, the accused was sentenced on each to four years imprisonment to run concurrently.

In sentencing the accused to life imprisonment for the killing of William Johnstone, the judge, Mr Justice Mocatta told him, 'For a man of your age you have a terrible record, and this in my judgement was a brutal murder.'

'It is apparent from your record that you resort to personal violence without any regard or mercy for those you attack. You have pleaded not guilty to the gravest crime in the criminal calendar and I have no alternative but to sentence you to life imprisonment.'

In relation to the other charges he said, 'Your brother and Mr Taylor were each doing their best in their own imperfect way to stop this' (how, in view of the evidence which had been presented, Judge Mocatta came to this conclusion is known only to himself), 'but all they got for their pains was a wound from you. It is obvious that your stabbing of them was needless and you were regardless of the consequences.'

# POSTSCRIPT

During the period since the turn of the twentieth century, there have been more than thirty-five deaths in the city of Leicester which, while they were not always recorded as murders, have certainly begun as murder enquiries. Of these, the most common source of the incident leading to the death of the person concerned has been based in a domestic environment – spur of the moment violence, an ongoing domestic dispute, infidelity, malice. Of the remainder, fights and drunken brawls account for the majority. Very few have been the stuff that the ubiquitous detective novel is made of. Consequently, only those that have some sort of a background story have been included in this volume.

The final case dealt with in Chapter 13 – the murder by John Crosbie of William Johnstone in 1966, coincides with the debate surrounding the abolition of capital punishment in this country, and as such, is probably an apposite cut-off point. The Murder (Abolition of Death Penalty) Act of 1965, was such a contentious piece of legislation that its implementation was held back for an experimental period until the end of 1969. On 16 December 1969, an all-party vote, supported for the government by the Prime Minister, Harold Wilson, and for the opposition parties, Edward Heath (Conservative), Jeremy Thorpe (Liberal), the continuance of the Act was held in the House of Commons where 343 members voted in support and 185 against. Two days later, the House of Lords also voted for the final acceptance of the Act and from that point onwards, capital punishment for the crime of murder in this country ceased.

Perhaps surprisingly, the calendar of executions for the crime of murder at Leicester Prison in the fifty years between 1903 and 1953, when Joseph Christopher Reynolds was to be the last man hanged there, is quite a slim one, totalling only eight men. (The last man to be hanged prior to the turn of the twentieth century was William Newell in December 1894 for murder at Loughborough.)

21 July 1903: Thomas Porter, for murder at Sileby.
21 July 1903: Thomas Preston, for murder at Sileby.
19 July 1911: William Henry Palmer, for murder at Walcote, near Lutterworth.
12 November 1914: Arnold Warren, for murder at Leicester.
23 December 1941: Thomas William Thorpe, for murder at Leicester.
8 August 1944: William Frederick George Meffen, for murder at Chaddesdon, Derby.

8 Aug 1944: William Alfred Cowle, for murder at Leicester.

17 November 1953: Joseph Christopher Reynolds, for murder at Leicester.

Until the middle of the nineteenth century, the sanction of the law was viewed not only as something which should be done, but which should also be seen to be done, and as such, the executions of criminals were conducted in the full view of the public.

From 5 a.m. on the morning of Friday 10 August 1832, the day set aside for the execution of James Cook for the murder of John Paas, crowds began to gather in the area outside the County Gaol on Welford Road. (The usual place for such executions was Infirmary Square, within walking distance of the gaol.) A few hours later at nine thirty – the appointed time for his execution – it was estimated that some 40,000 people had travelled into the town to witness the event.

The *Leicester Journal* describes the event in detail. 'At about half past nine, the culprit, proceeded by the Under Sheriff and clergyman, followed by the Town and County Gaoler, walked with a firm step to the drop.

'On coming out on the scaffold the unhappy culprit gazed intently around and waved his hand on recognising several former acquaintances. He appeared totally engaged in prayer and uttered the following pious ejaculation, "Lord remember me when thou come'st to judge the world."

'The rope was placed around his neck and he immediately threw away a white cambric pocket handkerchief. Everything being ready, the drop fell after considerable difficulty, and James Cook, the murderer, was very soon no more. He struggled violently for a space of about two minutes during which he gave some terrible convulsive heaves, and from the experience of an old officer who stood by, we are authorised in saying that he never witnessed a criminal die so hard. The crowd continued very orderly during the whole of the ceremony, several persons fainted away.

'He was dressed in a blue coat, black waistcoat, white gloves and trousers, holding in his left hand the handkerchief which Richards and Jeffery [the two constables who attended him during his confinement in the Borough Gaol] picked up according to an understanding they had while in prison, he shook hands very heartily with the town and county gaolers.

'After hanging the usual time, the body was taken down and put into chains pursuant to the sentence. The gibbet we understand will be erected in Saffron Lane, leading from the Aylestone toll gate to Countesthorpe, and within a quarter of a mile of the former place.'

Such was the notoriety attached to this execution that immediately the gibbet was set up, crowds gathered and a holiday atmosphere developed with stalls and throngs of people, to an extent that the town elders, fearing some sort of ensuing public disorder, hurriedly petitioned the Home office and were given permission to dismantle the gibbet in order to disperse the assembly.

The result of this distasteful show (an act intended to discourage others rather than to provide entertainment), was that Cook's corpse was the last to be displayed publicly in this manner.

If James Cook met his fate philosophically, this was not always to be the case. On 1 April 1846, William Hubbard, having been found guilty of the murder of his wife Hannah at Newarke on 11 August the previous year, was brought to the same place. A public handbill prepared after the event describes graphically what happened.

'From Saturday up to the hour of his execution the wretched man refused all assistance both temporal and spiritual. He was obliged to be held down while being shaved and on Tuesday began to kick at all who came near to him, so that they were obliged to chain his legs so that he could not move hand or foot, (it having been previously necessary to chain his hands), there he lay like a victim for the slaughter. (Hubbard says that the knife produced at the trial was not the one he used for the murder and that he had never seen it before, he having disposed of the one he used by dropping it into the mill dam near the floodgate.)

'On Wednesday morning before five o'clock straggling groups were moving towards the County Bridewell to witness the termination of the murderer's existence; and long previous to the appointed hour, Oxford Street, the spacious street leading to the scaffold was crowded with a dense living mass comprising a number of individuals not less than thirty thousand, among whom the utmost good order was manifested. At an early hour on Wednesday morning he was roused from his lethargy to prepare for his final doom – but was indifferent to the proceedings. He was conveyed in the prison van to the drop erected in front of the County Bridewell, when he was obliged to be assisted onto the scaffold and placed under the beam – the rope being soon adjusted and the cap placed over his eyes. The Chaplain reading the burial service, when as he said, "Lord have mercy upon us", the bolt was drawn and the wretched man was launched into eternity. The body after hanging for the usual time was conveyed back to the Borough Gaol and buried in a bricked grave eleven feet deep in the Debtors yard.'

Whatever the opinion of the individual with regards to what is or is not an appropriate punishment for the crime of murder – and there are many and differing, it has to be conceded that whether it be in a private execution chamber within the prison walls with only those whose presence is absolutely necessary – a hangman; prison officials to represent the judicial needs of the state; a priest for the spiritual needs of the prisoner and a doctor to afterwards certify death, or, as in days gone by when the condemned man was publicly hanged as a spectacle for all to witness, it is an act of ultimate finality.

# INDEX OF PEOPLE

McDowall 137–9
McGregor, James 57–8, 60–1
McGregor, Janice 57
McGurdy MP, C.A. 76
McMurdy MP, J. 53
Macaulay, Mr 27–30
Macauley, Dr 8
Makepeace, Gertrude 45, 47–8, 50–2
Malpighi, Marcello vii
Measures, Thomas 8, 10
Mee, Susan 18, 30
Meen, Reggie 43
Meffen, William F. 104
Mellor, Mr 28
Merson, Dr J.L. 99
Millard, Dr C.K. vii
Minto, Councillor John 79–80, 85
Minto, Mrs 79, 80
Mocatta, Justice 143
Moore, Dr C.W. 73, 75
Moore, PC 89
Murdy, Thomas 19, 30, 32
Myers, Thomas 101

Needham, George 83, 86
Newberry, Gordon A. 87
Newman, Pop 43
Nixon, Janice 109–10
Nokes, John 7, 8
Norman, Mr 49–50, 53
Norris, P. 84
North, Detective Inspector 59, 62–3
Noton, John 37–8, 40

Oliver, Justice 111
O'Riley, Dr James 136
Owston, George 10 11

Paas, John iv, 1–7, 10, 12, 14–16
Pallet, Mrs 57
Palmer, Thomas W. 20, 27, 31
Patterson, Justice v, 27, 29
Paull, Justice 124, 126

Payne, Frederick 96
Payne, Nora E. 95–103
Peel, Sir Robert 27
Pickering, Iris 79–86
Pickford, Justice 49,53, 55–6
Platts, William 37–9
Powers, G.W. 67
Pratt, Margaret 119
Priestley, Keith Frederick 117–125
Priestley, Kenneth 117
Prynne, Donald 74–5
Purkinje, John E. vii
Pym, Eric vi

Rafferty, R. 53
Rastenis, Adolfus 127–36
Rawson, Ald 8
Richardson, Jack 117
Riddngton, Roy 117–26
Rigley, Mrs 68
Rilett, Mr 128
Ritchie, John 137–41
Rose, Edward 67

Sanders, Joe 18
Sawbridge, John 3, 7
Sawbridge, Mary 6–7
Schuller, Dr 54
Shipman, PC 52
Singh, Avtar 106, 109, 111–14
Singh, Darshan 106–16
Singleton, Justice 99, 103
Skidmore, Elizabeth K. 72, 74–5
Slater, PC James 35
Smith, Catherine 18
Smith, Detective Inspector 59–60, 62, 64, 66, 69
Smith, Francis v
Smith, Mrs 108
Smith, Tacker 88
Spradbury, Ida M. 127–8, 130–3, 135–6
Spriggs, Neville I. 80, 84–5
Springthorpe, Sergeant Kenneth 100

Stallard, Dr John 24, 28
Stallard, Joshua H. 28
Stanley, Winifred E. 104
Stanton, Frederick 106–8
Stanton, Joyce 105–16
Stanyard, William 59, 60, 62–4, 68
Stanyon, Mrs 45
Stephens William W. 19, 27, 30
Stevens, Ann 43–56
Stevens, James 43–56
Studd, Brenda 142
Sutton, Mrs 79
Swanwick, G.R. 114
Sykes, Frank 87–93

Taylor, Annie 109
Taylor, Dr G.W. 98, 101–3
Taylor, Thomas 137–43
Tebbut, Richard 2, 5
Timson, Ann 28
Timson, John 8
Toone, Annie V. 127–31, 134–6

Ward, Arthur 99, 101
Ward, Dr Ernest M. 105, 123, 135
Ward, Edward 123
Ward, Miles 92
Waring, Mary 18, 20, 23–5, 28, 30, 32
Warren, Arnold iv, 71-8
Warren, Edith 71–2
Warren, James 1–3
Warren, Mary E. 72, 77
Watkinson, Charles 'Joe' 3
Watkinson, John vi
Watson, James 113
Wells, William H. 33–42
Weston, Mark 18
Wilcox, Dr William H. 66
Winning, Norman 92
Wisdich, Thomas 8, 13
Woods, David 141
Woods, PC John 99, 103
Woods, John W. 141